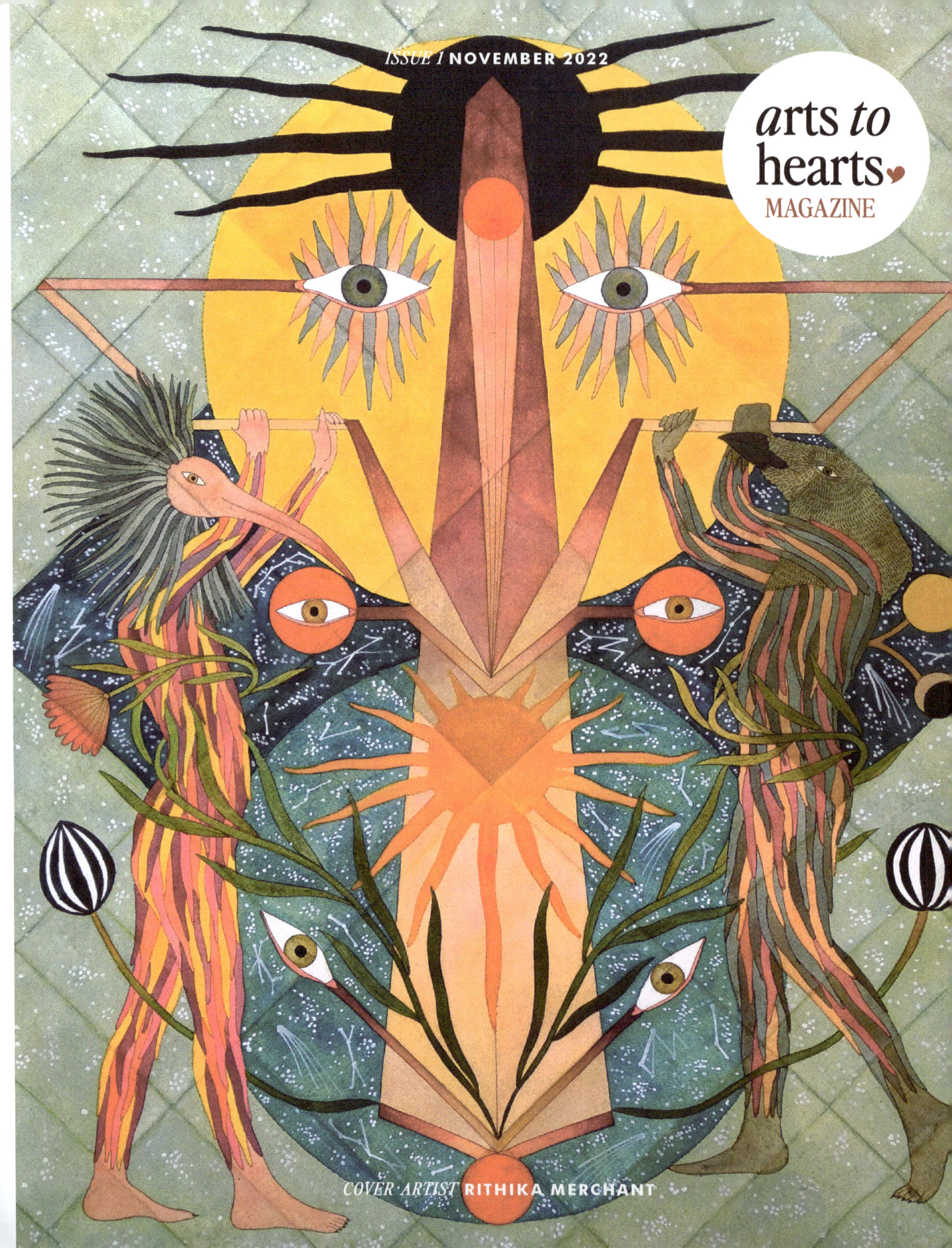

ISSUE 1 NOVEMBER 2022
arts to hearts
MAGAZINE
COVER ARTIST RITHIKA MERCHANT

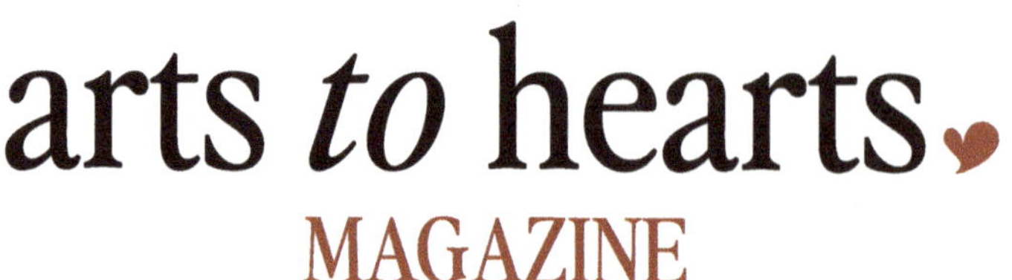

An Art publication with a mission to
Discover, Connect, and Engage with
Contemporary & Emerging Women Artists
From around the world.

A Product of

ARTS TO HEARTS PROJECT

We are a global creative community uniting contemporary & emerging women Artists to build successful, fulfilling, and money-making careers via collaboration, learning, community, networking, and peer-to-peer learning.

SUBMIT YOUR WORK

We have several opportunities throughout the year for people interested in the global arts. From open calls to grants to exhibits, you can stay on top of all our upcoming and ongoing opportunities by subscribing to our newsletter on our website.

COVER ART

Rithika Merchant | Monument to Us, 2022
65 x 50 cms / 25.5 x 19.6 in
Gouache, watercolour and ink paper.

JOIN WOMEN ARTISTS WORLD WIDE BY ATH
www.facebook.com/groups/
womenartistsworldwideath/

VISIT OUR WEBSITE
www.artstoheartsproject.com

FOLLOW US ON INSTAGRAM
@artstoheartsproject

EMAIL
info@artstoheartsproject.com

"I always tell visual artists to come up with an elevator pitch."

Don't just tell people what you do.
Tell why you do it and what makes it so
unique that you are doing this.

3

ATH Experts

Experts in the art world share their secrets to success and provide valuable advice on breaking and making it big in the art industry. In conversation with the Gallerist Hena Kapadia, TARQ gallery, Mumbai.

1

ATH Cover Artist

Join in the conversation as we speak to our cover artist Rithika Merchant as she takes us through her journey of the past five years of art production and the making of her first monograph.

6

ATH Asks

Learn about the perspectives and experiences of women artists from around the globe on art, 8, and the creative process.

4

Art Biz

In this session, we'll identify the next steps for you to take and help you develop reliable business procedures that will support your creative growth. The article will teach you how to choose a price for your artwork that will bring in the most money.

2

ATH Shop

Easily customizable plug & play templates perfect for beginners to advanced artists looking to up their game. A perfect way to get started in the world of art. From studio planner, invoicing to portfolio templates everything on shop.artstoheartsproject.com

7

ATH Curated Artists

Learn all about the work, process, and inspiration of the curated artists from all around the world by digging into their creative journey.

5

Creative Inspiration

While it's true that creative people tend to think similarly, this will give you fresh perspectives and new ideas from women artists worldwide.

EDITOR:
Charuka Arora

CONTRIBUTORS WRITERS:
Juliana Naufel
Volta Voloshin-Smith
Laurén Brady
Rabia Khan

LEAD DESIGNER:
Sikandar Khan

FIND US ON:
www.artstoheartsproject.com
https://www.facebook.com/groups/womenartistsworldwideath/
instagram.com/artstoheartsproject

GENERAL ENQUIRIES:
info@artstoheartsproject.com

**READ OUR DIGITAL
EDITORIALS AND
RESOURCES ON:**
www.artstoheartsproject.com

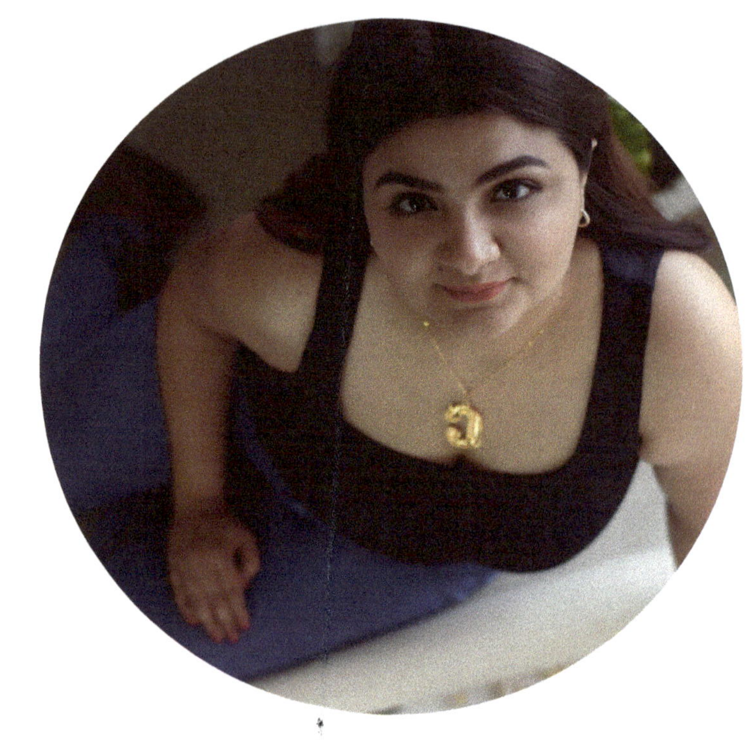

Editor's Note

Dear Reader, A new path. A collective voice. A new story. A safe, intimate space for women in the arts to connect and grow is what I envision as I write this to you for our first-ever issue of the ATH Magazine. I am so thrilled to be sharing this empowering and honest issue with you that deep dives into the lives of our women artists. A dream is now a reality. That houses some incredibly talented women from around the world in this issue.

Setting the tone with the cover artwork 'A moment to us' by Rithika Merchant, followed by a candid conversation with her, to talking to gallerist Hena Kapadia about her vision and work in the art world, we have started with a bang. Not only that, our writers discuss art pricing, artist dates, and interviews with artists from across cultures.

As you read on this issue, there is much to discover and engage. As artists in our curated section share their deep-down fears to zone of genius, there is no holding back. I am incredibly grateful to our team of writers, designers, and artists for making this issue memorable. And truly making a mark. Get your seats together because *"HERE ARE THE WOMEN ARTISTS"* and we are here to stay.

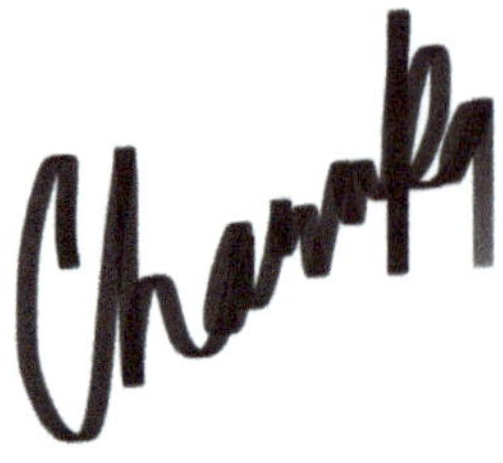

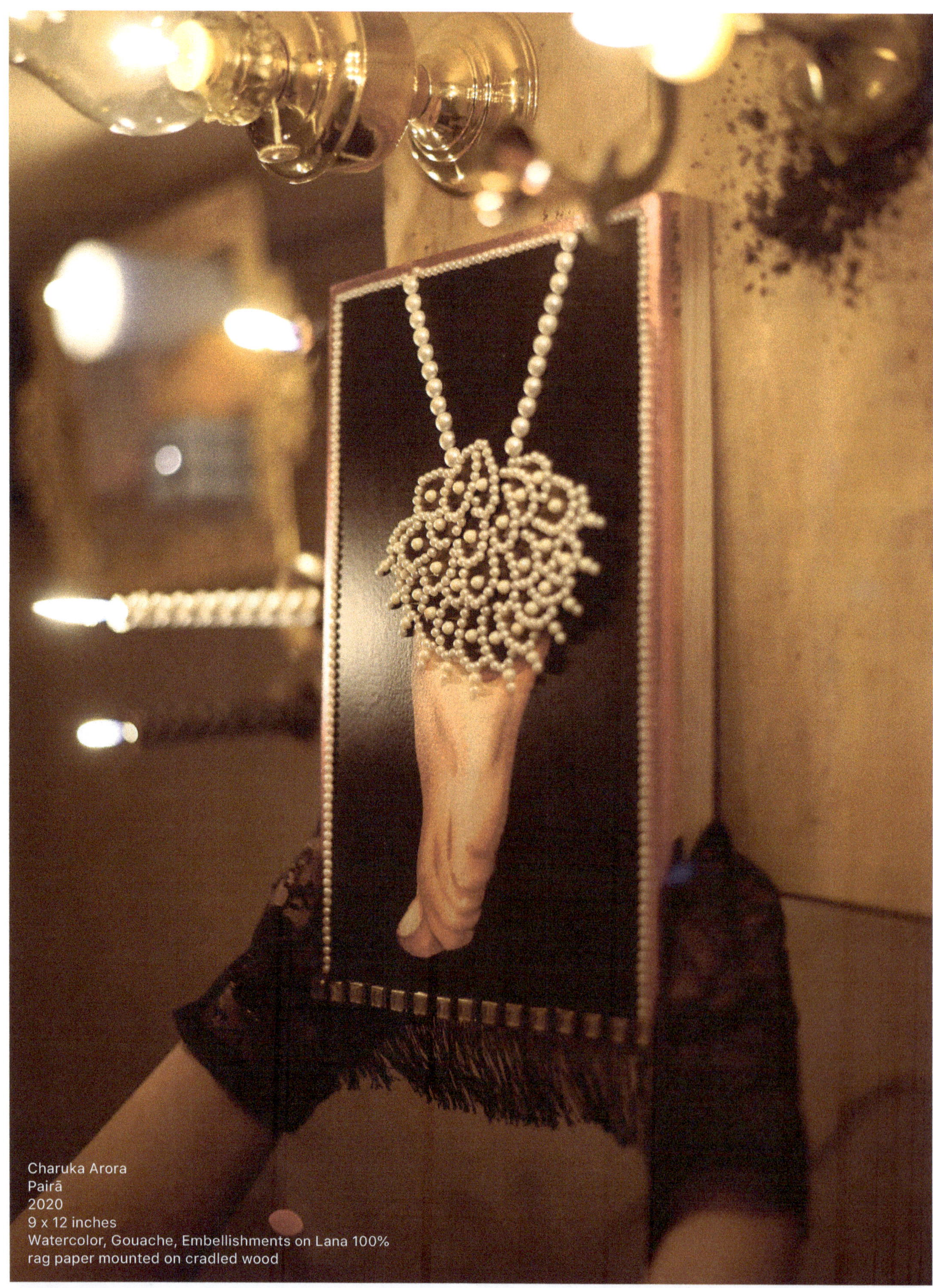

Charuka Arora
Pairā
2020
9 x 12 inches
Watercolor, Gouache, Embellishments on Lana 100%
rag paper mounted on cradled wood

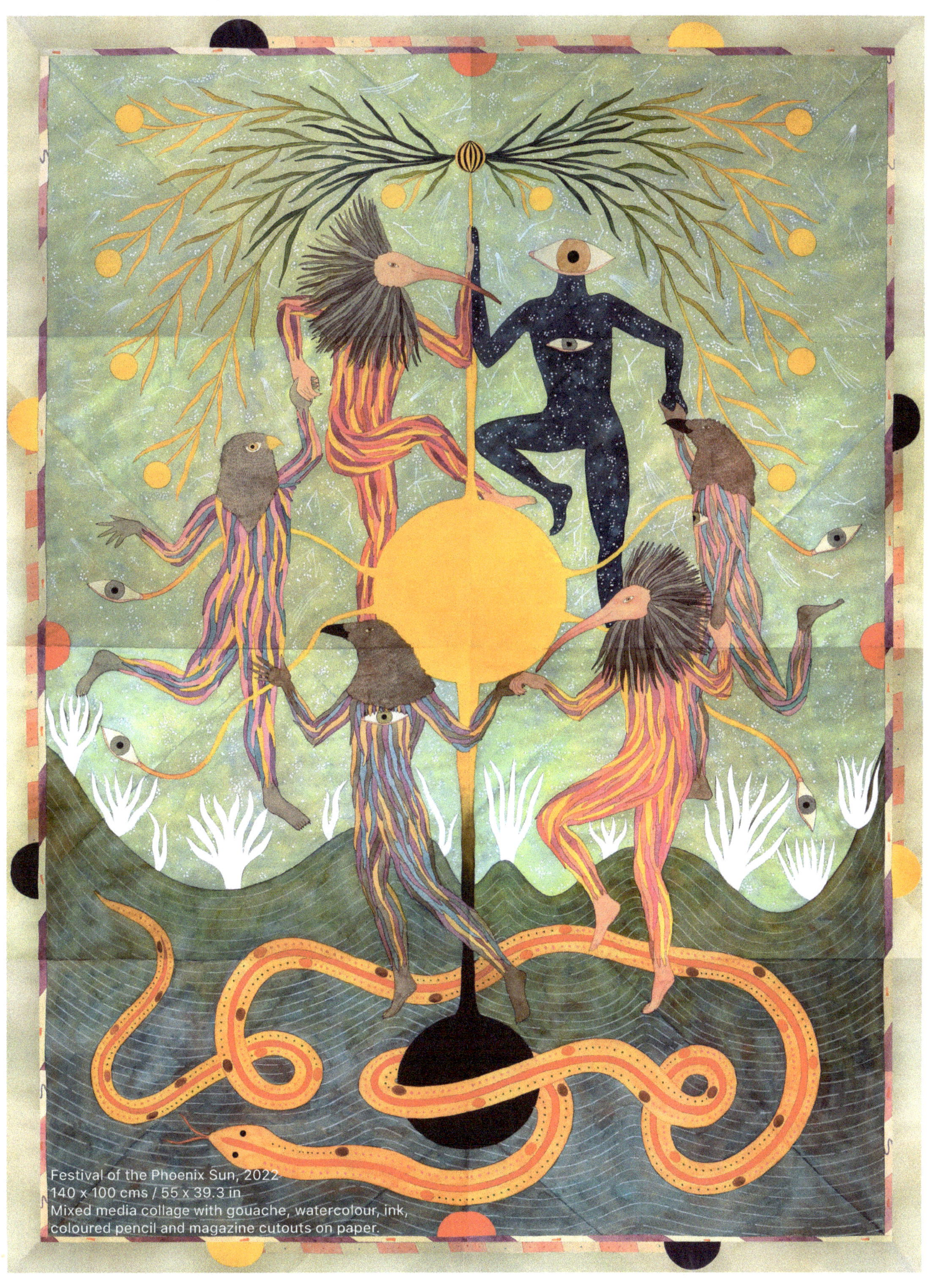

Festival of the Phoenix Sun, 2022
140 x 100 cms / 55 x 39.3 in
Mixed media collage with gouache, watercolour, ink,
coloured pencil and magazine cutouts on paper.

Meet RITHIKA MERCHANT

Our Cover artist

Interview by Charuka Arora

Rithika Merchant is a visual artist from Bombay (Mumbai), India. Her work explores the common thread that runs through different cultures and religions. Similar myths, stories and ideas are shared by cultures all around the world, her paintings explore this concept while also featuring creatures and symbolism that are part of her personal visual vocabulary.

Nature plays a pivotal role in her work and is emphasised by the use of organic shapes and non saturated colours. Her paintings and collages are made using a combination of watercolour and cut paper elements, drawing on 17th century botanical prints and folk art, to create a body of work that is visually linked to our collective pasts.

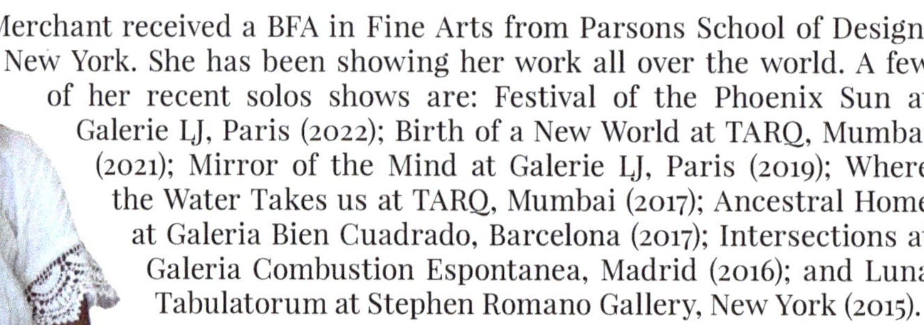

Merchant received a BFA in Fine Arts from Parsons School of Design, New York. She has been showing her work all over the world. A few of her recent solos shows are: Festival of the Phoenix Sun at Galerie LJ, Paris (2022); Birth of a New World at TARQ, Mumbai (2021); Mirror of the Mind at Galerie LJ, Paris (2019); Where the Water Takes us at TARQ, Mumbai (2017); Ancestral Home at Galeria Bien Cuadrado, Barcelona (2017); Intersections at Galeria Combustion Espontanea, Madrid (2016); and Luna Tabulatorum at Stephen Romano Gallery, New York (2015).

Merchant collaborated with Chloé, a French fashion house on multiple collections for which she was awarded the Vogue India Young Achiever of the Year Award at its Women of the Year Awards 2018, as well as named one of Vogue Magazine's VogueWorld 100 Creative Voices. She is also the winner of the Sovereign Asian Art Prize 2021 - Vogue.

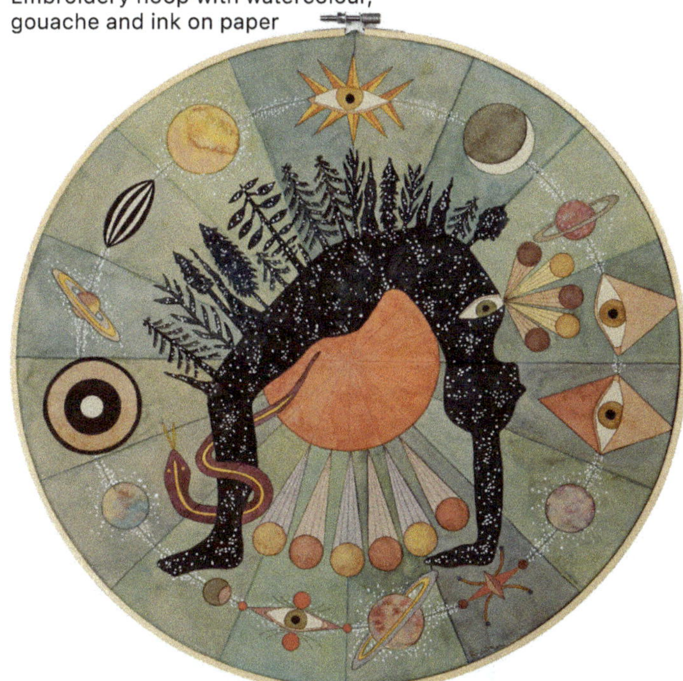

Vega, 2021
16.5 x 16.5 in
Embroidery hoop with watercolour,
gouache and ink on paper

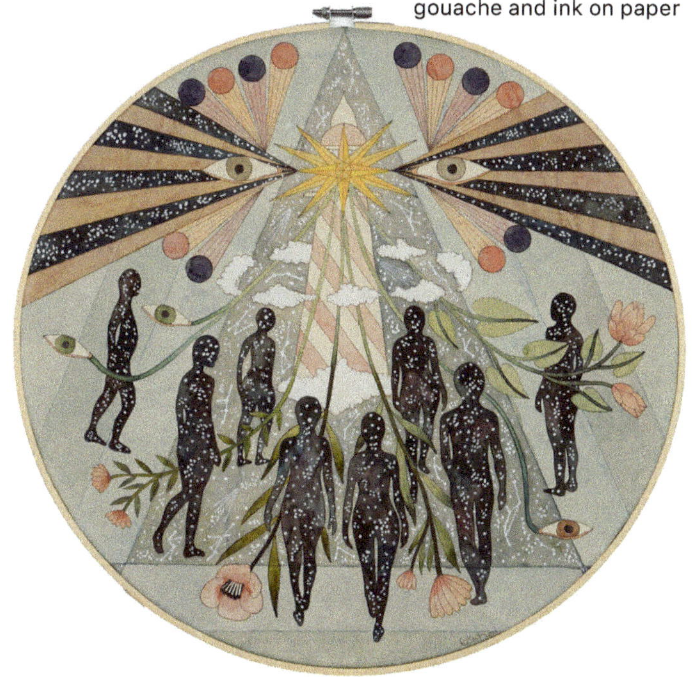

Vela, 2021
16.5 x 16.5 in
Embroidery hoop with watercolour,
gouache and ink on paper

So Rithika, can you tell us a little bit more about your recent project 'The Eye, The Sky, The Altar'? It's your first monograph, correct? Can you tell us a little bit more about your works and practice from these past years?

This is my first monograph and I'm very excited about it! It's a look at the last 4 to 5 years of production and it's a nice overview of how my work has evolved during that period of time. It also includes a conversation with Fariha Róisín. She's a writer and a dear friend - it's a casual, quite insightful conversation. It feels like a bit of a career milestone to to have a book. The book itself is so beautifully designed - we worked with Zeenat Kulavoor at Bombay Duck Designs and she designed this incredible book which ended up being a beautiful art object.

What have you enjoyed the most about this collaborative creative project? How do you think your experience has been about it?

I loved it because I worked with Hena from TARQ, Adeline from Galerie LJ and Zeenat from Bombay Duck Designs. The main creators of the project are all women, so that its very special to me. Working with three incredible women made me grateful for community aspect of it. All our little zoom meetings, sitting together and planning are so dear to me. I just loved working with all these inspiring and strong women to put this project out in the world. The creative experience working with people that you feel very aligned with is also very fulfilling.

What has it felt like looking back at your work produced in the past 4-5 years?

It feels...affirming. It's kind of nice to look back on the past few years of work and see all of the work that I've made. I try to be really present while I'm making the work, and often before I've absorbed it fully once it's done - the works go to exhibitions then I just never see them again. So it makes me feel accomplished to look back on it all and see it all in one place.

Can you see your journey or how you evolved as an artist with all these works in the monograph? Do you see any kind of connection or story that you feel marks you?

The monograph has been arranged according to themes rather than chronologically. So for example, like there's a section that's just collages, one for "altars and talismans" etc.

It's been interesting to see how symbolism has evolved in my work. It's been really cool to look back at what I was thinking about when I made those works at the time and where I was in my own creative journey. The way the book is arranged is also going to give the reader more insight into that as well.

We are thrilled to have you as the cover artist for our magazine's first 'Invite only' issue with the theme 'Here are the women artists'. Can you tell me a little bit about your journey as a woman in the arts? How has that been so far?

What's your intention for this monograph?
What do you want people to experience through it?

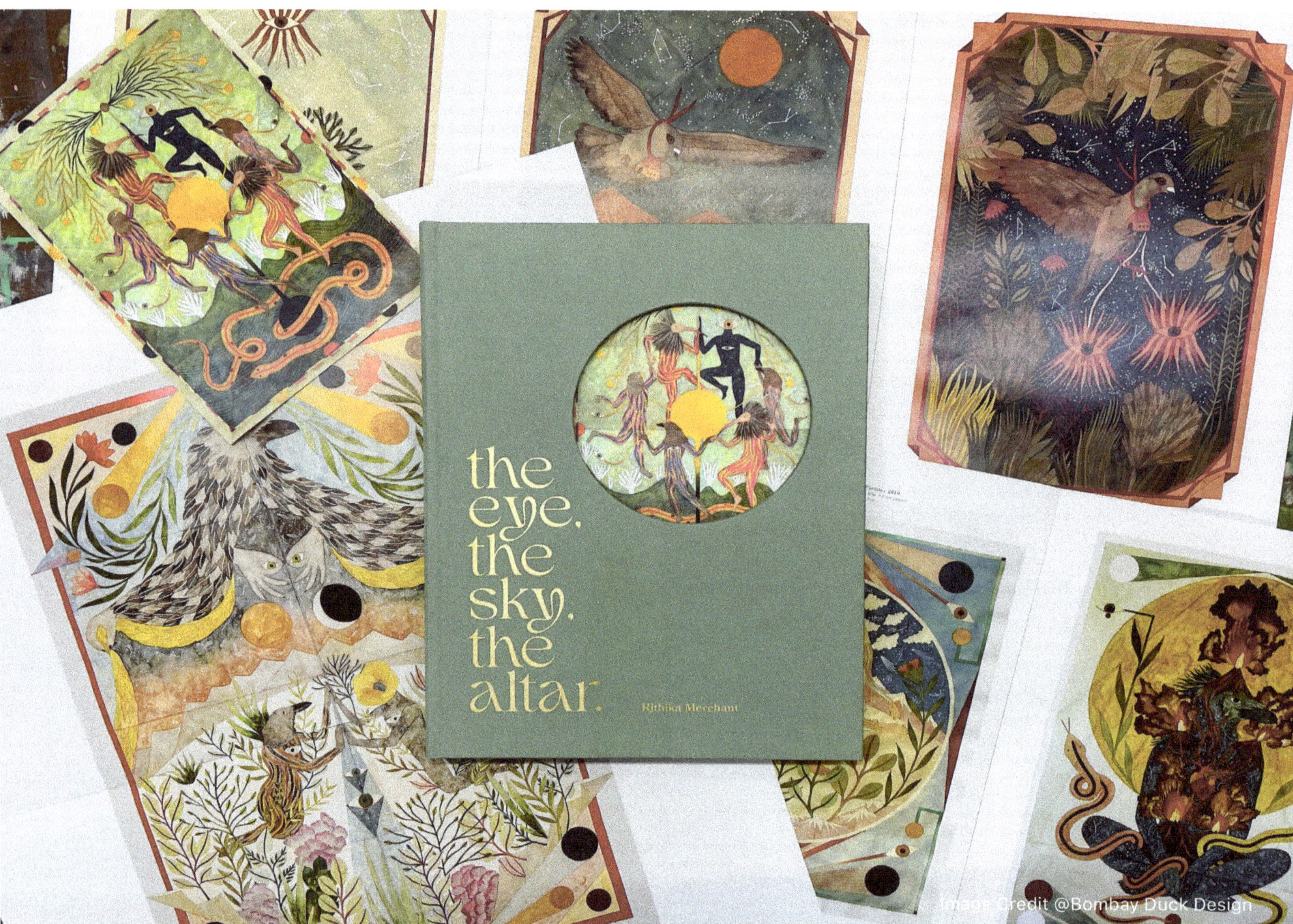

It's turned into a beautiful art object. So, in many ways it's a great way for my audience and people who have followed my work for a long time to actually almost have a piece of my art in their home. It's a lot more affordable than my paintings. It also gives so much more insight into my creative journey. I don't really talk that much about it and you only get so much when you follow someone online or if you go and see an exhibition. So having everything together will give a lot more understanding of me as an artist.

Her work has been written about in The New York Times, The Huffington Post, Vogue, Elle, Harpers Bazaar, Verve Magazine, The Hindu, The Indian Express, Hyperallergic, Architectural Digest, and others. Merchants work is held in public and private collections including the Chloe Archive, Palais Galliera, Musée de la mode de la Ville de Paris, Collection de Bueil & Ract-Madoux and The Sarmaya Arts Foundation.

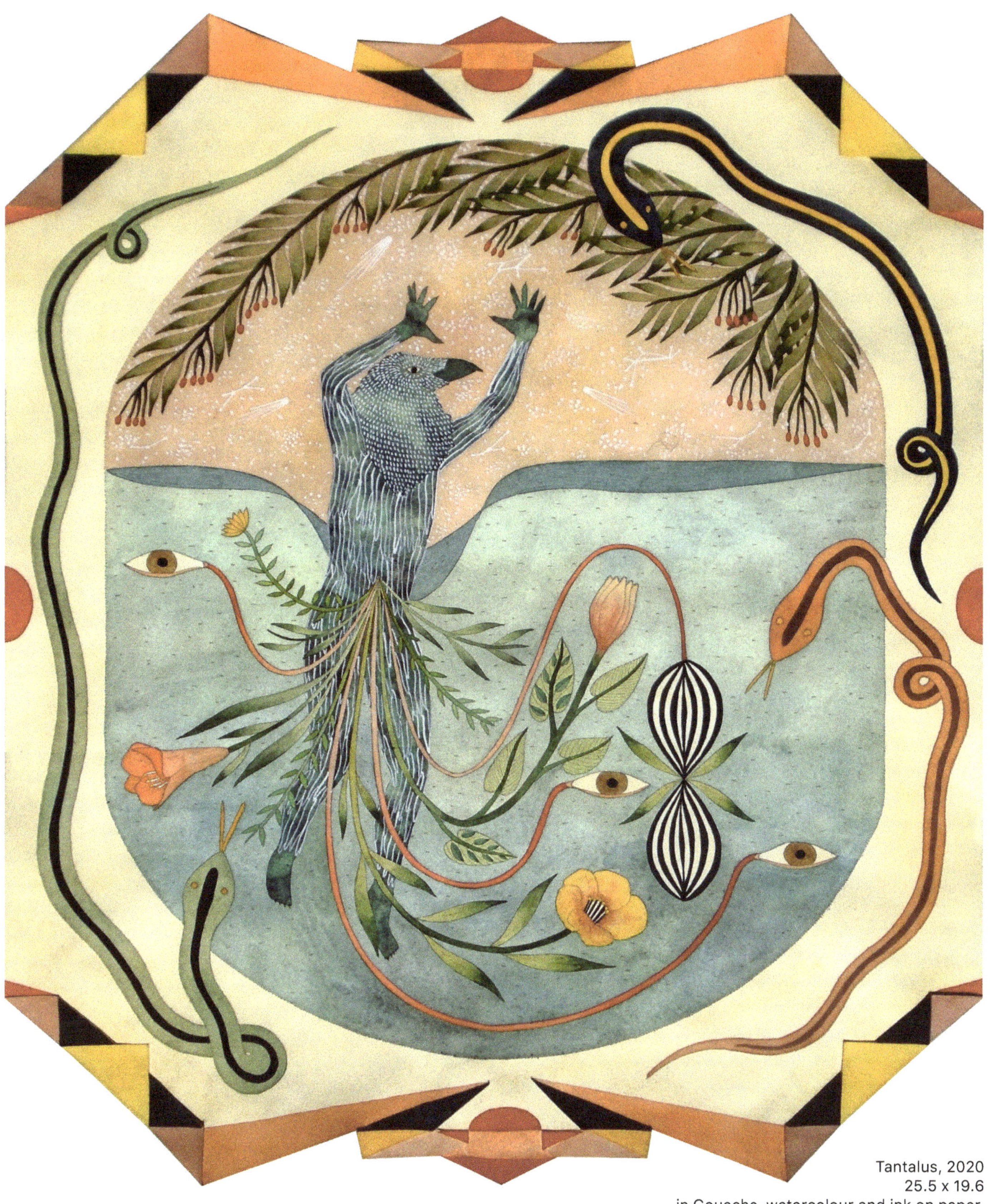

Tantalus, 2020
25.5 x 19.6
in Gouache, watercolour and ink on paper.

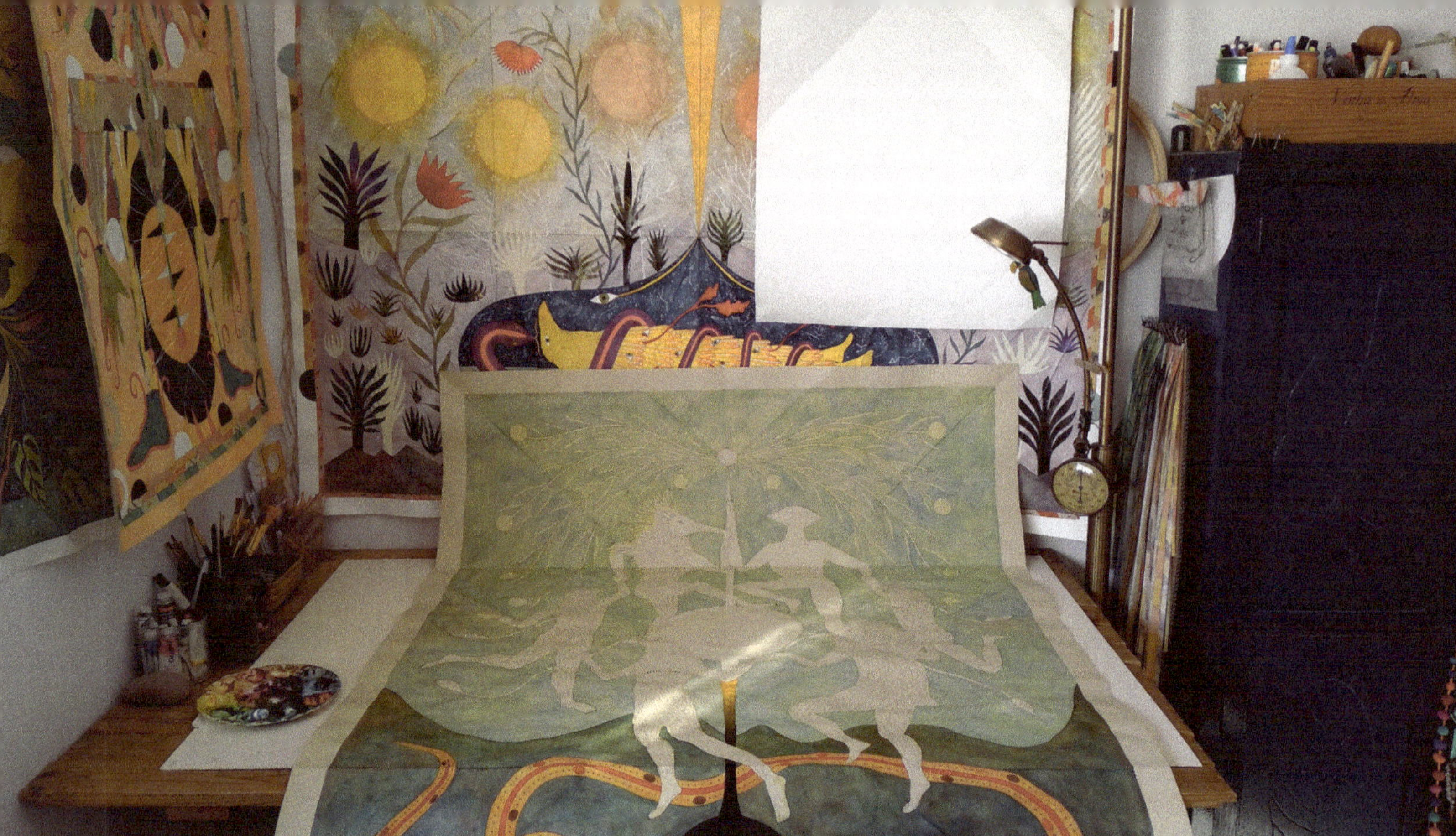

It's lovely to see that you respond to my work so much - I am very grateful and excited to be the cover artist. We have made a bit of a friendship through the podcast and our conversations after that, so thank you for including me in this!

In terms of my journey, I feel like I have been really lucky and also for most part I've worked with other women. It's been really good honestly, especially as a young artist I've always felt very safe with the other creative women. Hena and I have in many ways almost grown up together. We've gone through so many phases of the gallery and my career together. Just having another woman support me through all of it has been a very heartwarming experience.

What do you think has been your biggest struggle being a woman artist? Let's see what that comes up with.
I think the biggest - especially when I was younger - was feeling nervous to speak up . I have also talked about this in my podcast interview with you on the Arts to Hearts Podcast. I was raise by parents who always taught me to speak up, but I do remember feeling quite nervous at the beginning of my career. Also, learning to set boundaries - which I have gotten pretty good with now.

What's that one advice that you would like to give to other emerging women artists who are reading this right now?
I would say to commit yourself deeply to your craft because that's the best piece of advice I've personally gotten. And, Consistency is key. That's the advice that I was given and it's advice that I've followed and I feel like it has gotten me quite far.

One last question before I let you go - what's coming next for you? What are you working on that you can share with us?
I'm going to Senegal in the month of November for a one month artist residency. I'm very excited about that I'm looking forward to seeing how this new place is going to influence my work. I plan to engage with the local community and learn more about the folklore and the mythology of the land. I'm really really looking forward to that!

I've got a solo show coming up next year in London at Kristin Hjellegjerde Gallery so I'm in the midst of working on that as well.

Are you an Artist Who wants to Sell your work?

With these easily customizable plug & play templates, you can start selling your art like a pro. So what are you waiting for? Grab your Artist Brand Pack now and get started on your journey to success.

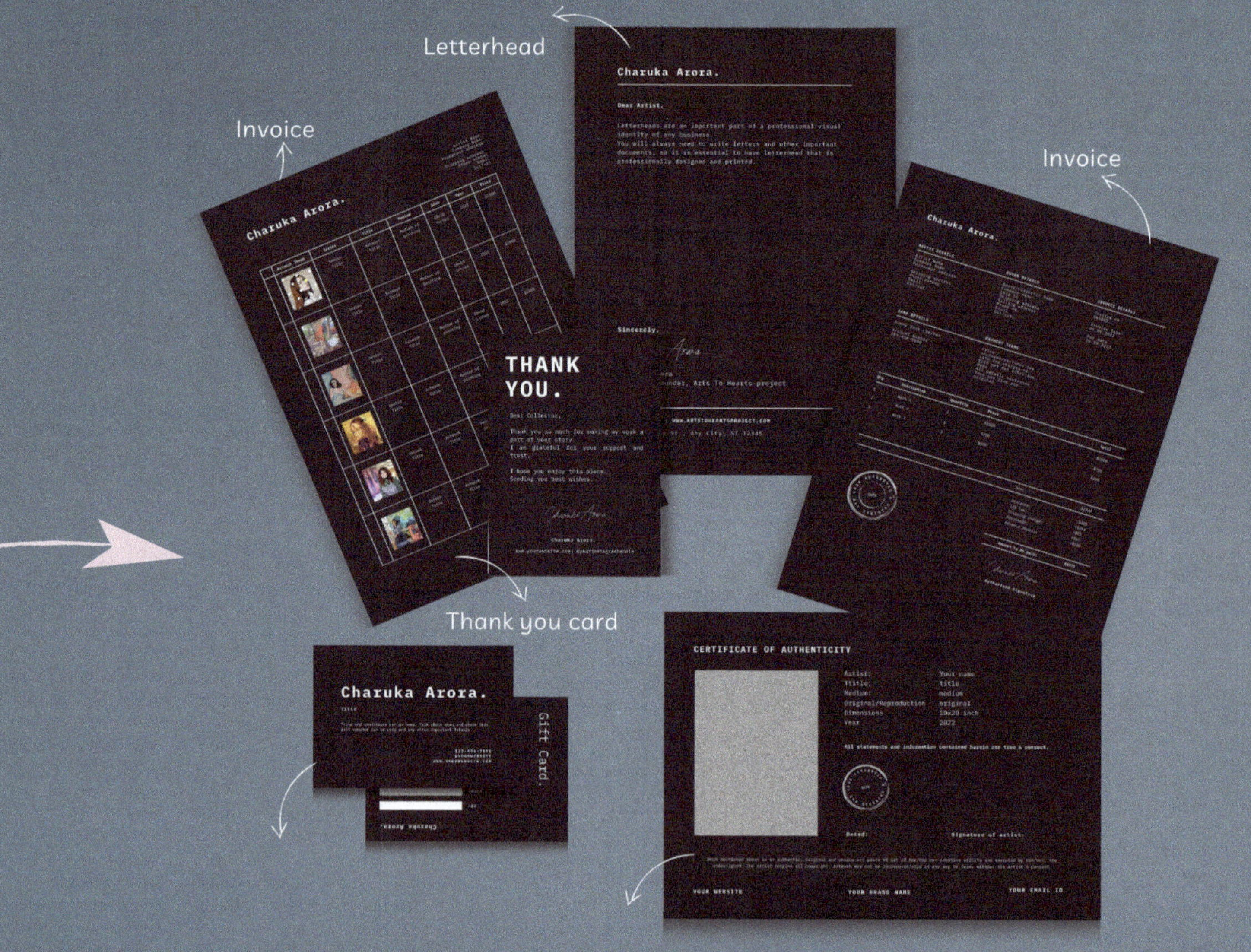

The Artist Brand Pack is a great way to get started in the world of art sales. It includes everything you need to get started.

It Includes a gift card, thank you card, invoice template, image list, authenticity certificate, and letterhead. Plus, a bonus brand card is included for good measure.

Shop Your Artist Brand Pack Now on,

shop.artstoheartsproject.com

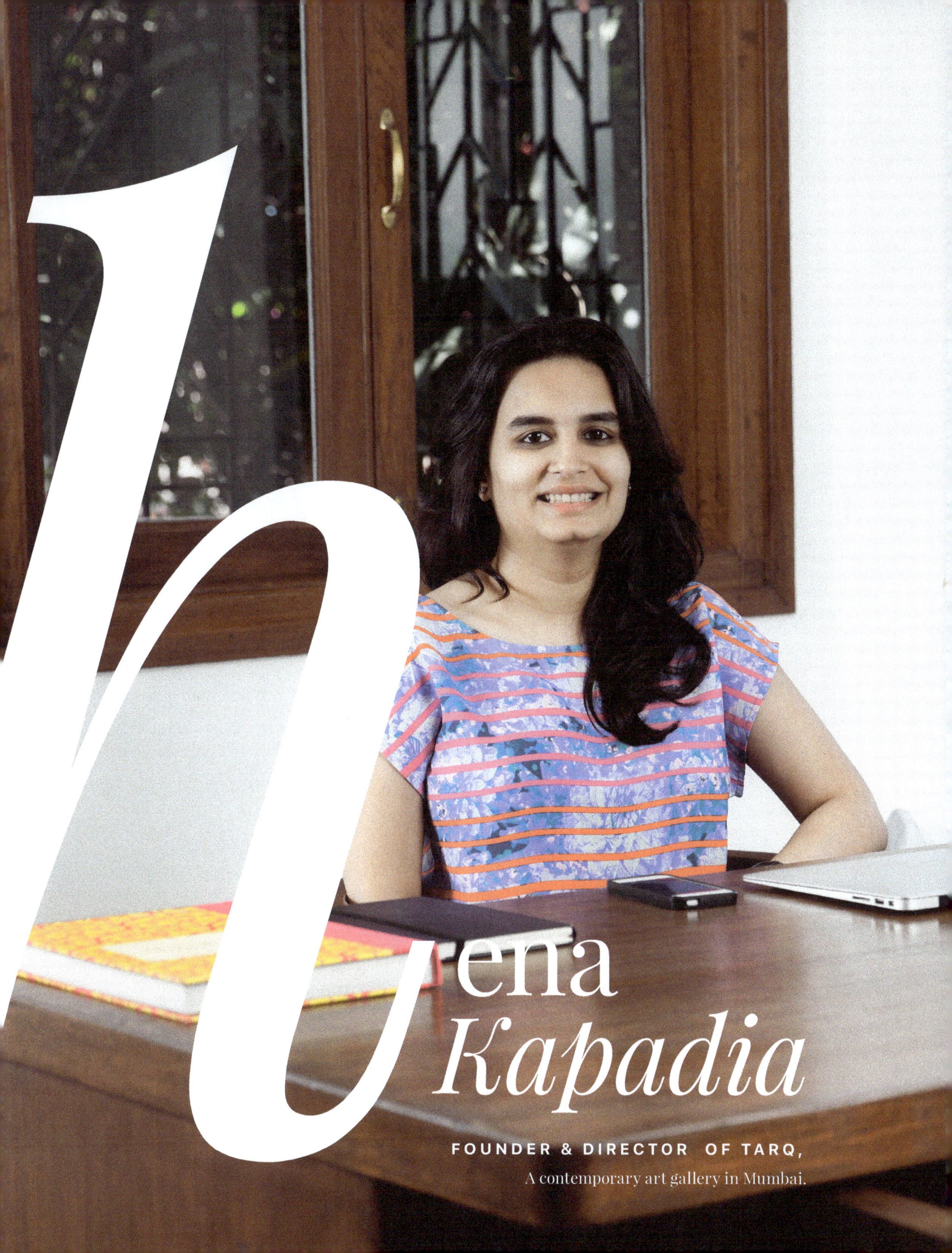

*b*ena *Kapadia*

In CONVERSATION *with a* GALLERIST

Interview by Charuka Arora

Edited by Rabia Khan

Hena Kapadia is the founder and gallery director of TARQ, a contemporary art gallery in Mumbai. After majoring in Art History and Economics at Tufts University in Massachusetts, she completed her Master's Degree in Modern and Contemporary Art World Practice at Christie's Education, the University of Glasgow in London.

At TARQ, she focuses on exhibiting and engaging with process-driven and thought-provoking artists. A fundamental interest of her practice is maintaining close relationships with artists and patrons and encouraging thoughtful art acquisitions. Apart from TARQ's regular shows, the gallery is committed to building an educational structure that enables the art community to grow through discussion, debate, and dialogue across various fields.

TARQ was founded in 2014 by Hena Kapadia on the value of creating a meaningful conversation around art and its myriad connotations and contexts. It was envisioned as a laboratory - an incubator for young contemporary artists which would work towards pushing the boundaries of how contemporary art in India is exhibited and perceived. TARQ's youthful and experimental ethos encourages collectors, novice and seasoned alike, to approach art collecting through a perspective that marries thoughtfulness with a curious eye for aesthetics and artistic processes.

Since its conception, TARQ has endeavored to create a robust outreach program that ties in with the gallery's exhibitions and overall raison d'être. The program is an amalgam of educational initiatives in workshops, gallery walk-throughs, and talks. They intend to engage with a diverse audience to develop an informed viewership for contemporary art in the future.

Okay, Let's start with why did you decide to run an Art gallery?

I opened the gallery because I wanted to facilitate discussions about art. Art, in my opinion, is a two-way street meant to spark debates, arguments and discussions. The plan was to promote artists from my own generation and also build a collector base of that same generation. In that way, they can interact with young artists from the start of their careers. I also wanted to create a safe space for people to learn about art. Many of our collectors are first-time buyers, and we want them to feel comfortable and excited about the artwork and artist that they're looking at. We're also now in a stage where we're getting to do second and third solo shows with our artists so watching them grow has been very exciting for me.

As a gallerist, you often act as a link between art collectors and creatives. How would you describe this role?

I understand that sometimes it's challenging for the artists to put themselves out there and speak about their works, but I see this as a very important aspect of the job. We keep encouraging our artists to talk about their own work themselves, because I think that no one can do this better than the artist themselves. For me, there's nothing better than watching an artist and collector interact. It's a testament to them and their work and them pushing themselves into a place where they're happy to engage with collectors.

OK, so this piqued my interest, and I was wondering when and how you first began serving the arts. No one ever says, "Today I will become a gallerist," so please tell us about your background.

My mother is an art historian so whenever we traveled I was always taken to visit museums and galleries. At first, this was against my will but then I realized that this is something I really enjoy. I also had the opportunity to be an intern at Geetha Mehra's Sakshi Gallery which was a pivotal experience for me. While I was there they were working on Jehangir Sabavala's retrospective and catalogue so I was able to interact with him and go to his studio which was wonderful for me. This experience of being at Sakshi Gallery made me decide that this is something I want to do.

What do you think needs to improve in the Indian art ecosystem?

When Indians go abroad they actively seek out museums and galleries but don't do the same in India. I think the education system and the lack of institutional support is where this lack of curiosity stems from. I read a report on government spending recently where they had allotted a very small amount to art under the umbrella of art, culture, tourism. A lot of this money goes to the performing arts, not that those areas don't need money, but contemporary art then often gets overlooked. Contemporary art is a billion-dollar industry so I think there's a lot of scope for growth and development.

What is your opinion on the visibility women artists get in India?

There are more opportunities for women now than there were before. I think this is also reflected in our roster of artists where we have more women than men at this point.

Tell me something, how did the pandemic impact the gallery? How you as a gallery coped up with the changing times?

For me, community is at the core of what we do so sustaining and growing our community during the pandemic was very important to me. Our presence shifted online and we did a few online shows and zoom events that helped us engage with a more global community. After we came back and started doing events in person again we had people in the gallery that I had never seen before saying that they love our work. This was so fulfilling to hear because it meant that we had been successful in building a community online, something that I hadn't thought was possible before. Having people in the gallery was something that I really missed during the pandemic.

Okay, what has been the most challenging aspect of your eight years as a gallerist & a creative entrepreneur?

For me, the hardest has been balancing work and family. Especially after having a child. There are certain expectations that I have to deal with, but apart from that it's been great. Every difficult situation has been overcome and I've been able to learn from it.

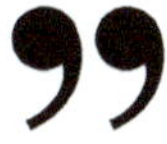

> *There are more opportunities for women now than there were before.*

You've established yourself, and your gallery is among one of India's best. What are your hopes for the future of your gallery?

I want to keep growing. I think what I've done well is build a local community so I want to keep building on that. Simultaneously I want to make sure that my artists get the international exposure that they deserve, so we're working on that as well.

That's fantastic to hear. To wrap up, I'd like to know what piece of advice you'd provide to an up-and-coming artist who hopes to one day be acknowledged for their work.

For me, practice is the most important. How do you make your work and why? I think it's also important to get to know the galleries, figure out if you like the gallerist, and if your work fits with their program before you share your work with them. It's vital to do your research before you share your work so that you can increase your chances of your work being acknowledged.

Do you want to get the most out of your creative practice?

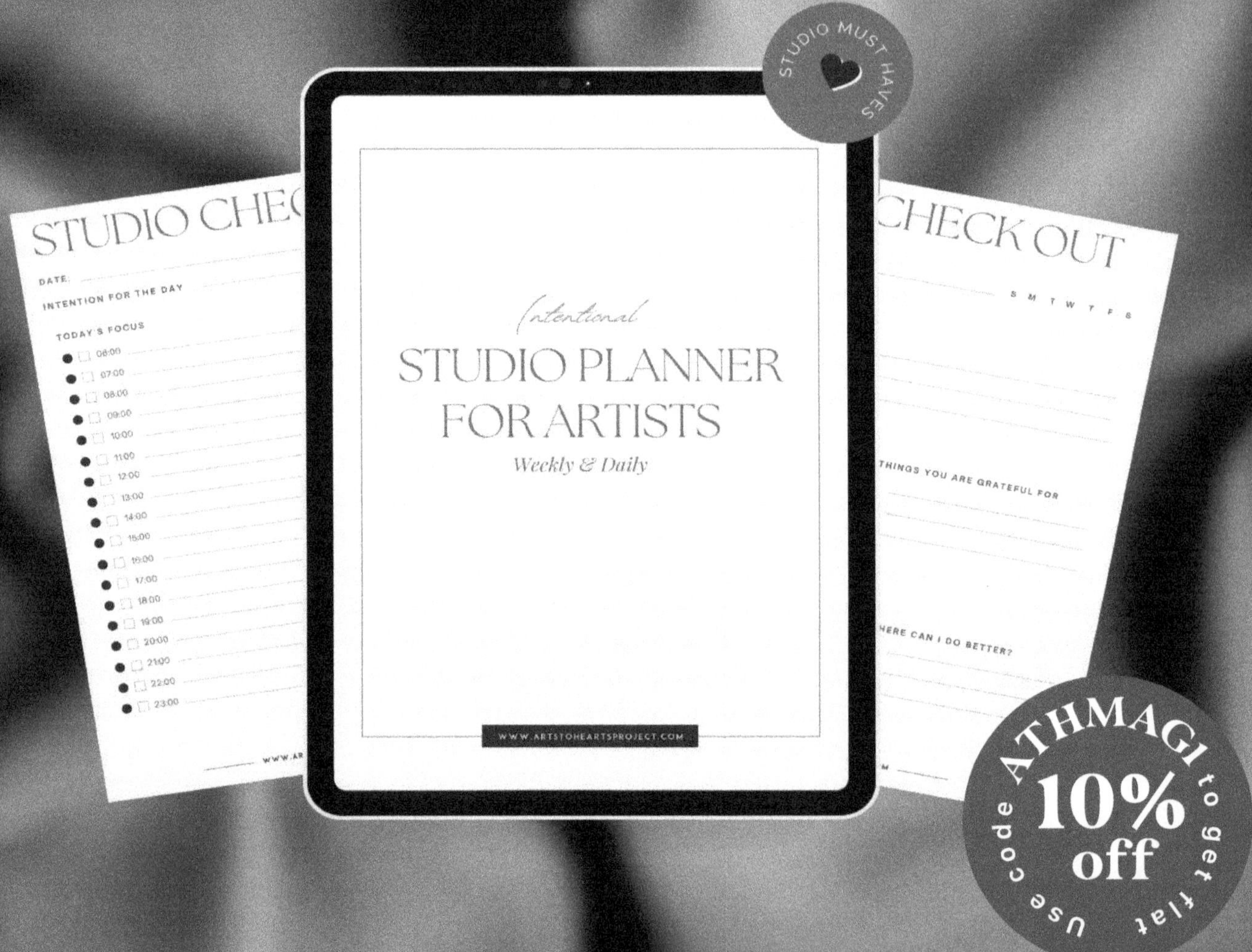

The Studio Planner for Artists is the perfect way to plan your week.
This planner includes everything you need to create your to do list,
Track your things to get done, and track your progress with studio
check in and check out and a space to dump your creative ideas.
It is undated so you can start using it at any time, and it has plenty
of space for you to write down your thoughts and ideas.

Get your own Studio Planner for Artists today!

shop.artstoheartsproject.com

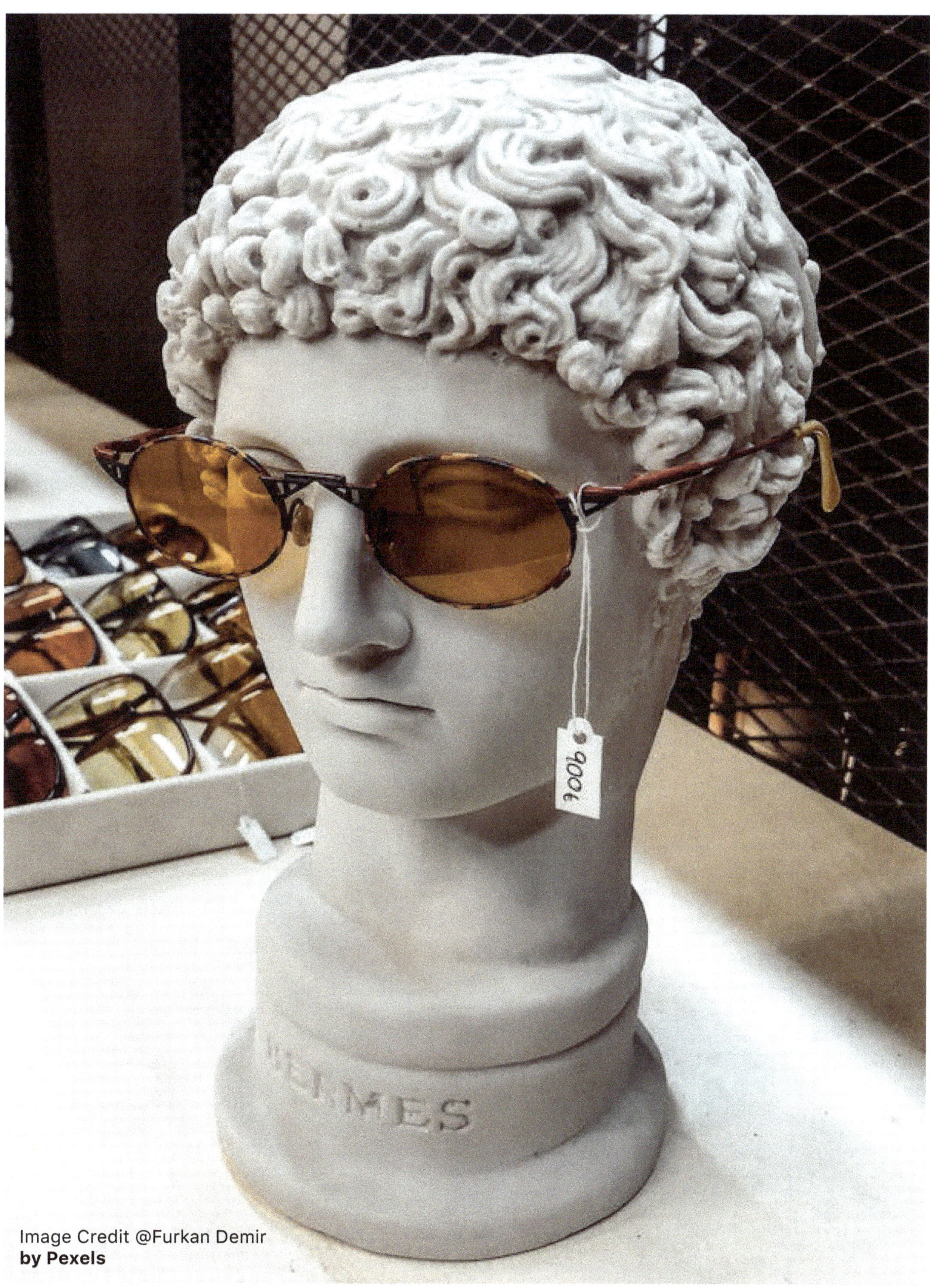

Image Credit @Furkan Demir
by Pexels

How to Price Your *Art* for Maximum *Profit*

Written by Rabia Khan

Let's be honest: as artists, we all hope to sell our creations and artworks for a premium price. After all, many steps are involved in making a piece of art, from choosing a topic to working out the details of the composition to selecting the appropriate medium to finally choosing the right frame. So much of our time and effort goes into dealing with all this.

And when we finally build up the nerve to offer our creations for sale, we confront the issue of how to best set prices for our artwork.

So if you want to learn how to price your art for maximum profit, then keep reading.

It's essential to maintain an accurate accounting of your spending

Determining a fair price for a work of art is analogous to the time required to complete it. You must realize that there is no one set formula for setting the value of your artwork and that various artists employ various strategies. But, the first step in determining a fair price for your artwork is to keep a record of all the money and time you have put into it.

When setting a price for your artwork, you should include the entire cost of materials. In determining your price, it is crucial to factor in the cost of materials like cardboard, paper, colors, brush, packing material, etc. So, calculate how much you've spent on materials and other expenses to create the artwork, and set the price accordingly to maximize your earnings.

Analyze Your Customer Base

Nowadays, it's much simpler to sell one's work all over the world because of the widespread availability of the internet. Almost all creative professionals today have e-shops where they may showcase and sell their work. In light of this, you should research to find out more about the kinds of people who might be interested in your work.

You can easily set a fair price for your product once you have researched your customer base. This research of the customer base will help you determine the maximum price at which your clientele will purchase a specific work of art.

Decide Where You Will Sell You Art

Many artists set the selling price of their artwork only after they've determined how they'll sell it. They do this because the cost of the gallery's fee needs to be factored into the selling price of the artwork if you decide to sell it through the gallery.

So consider how and where you would like to market your artwork. Can you envision yourself selling your artwork at a gallery show, a fair, or an online store? After deciding that, take the next step of pricing your art to get you maximum profit.

Take a look at what other artists are charging for similar work

Many artists do market research by comparing the ultimate prices of their work to those of other artists in the same sector. Before settling on a price, research the rates of other artists whose work is comparable to yours,

So by employing this strategy, you can establish pricing for your artwork that is in line with similarly skilled artists. Even if you're in a highly competitive market, this strategy will help you close the deal and turn a profit.

Think It Over, and Then Make a Choice You Won't Regret

Developing a sense of how much to charge for your artwork will take time, so don't rush the process if you're starting as a creative professional. Determine the optimal selling price for your creative work. Test out different prices to see what works best, and then adjust accordingly. Along with this, there are calculators available on the internet that can help you finalize the final cost of your artwork, so do give it a try.

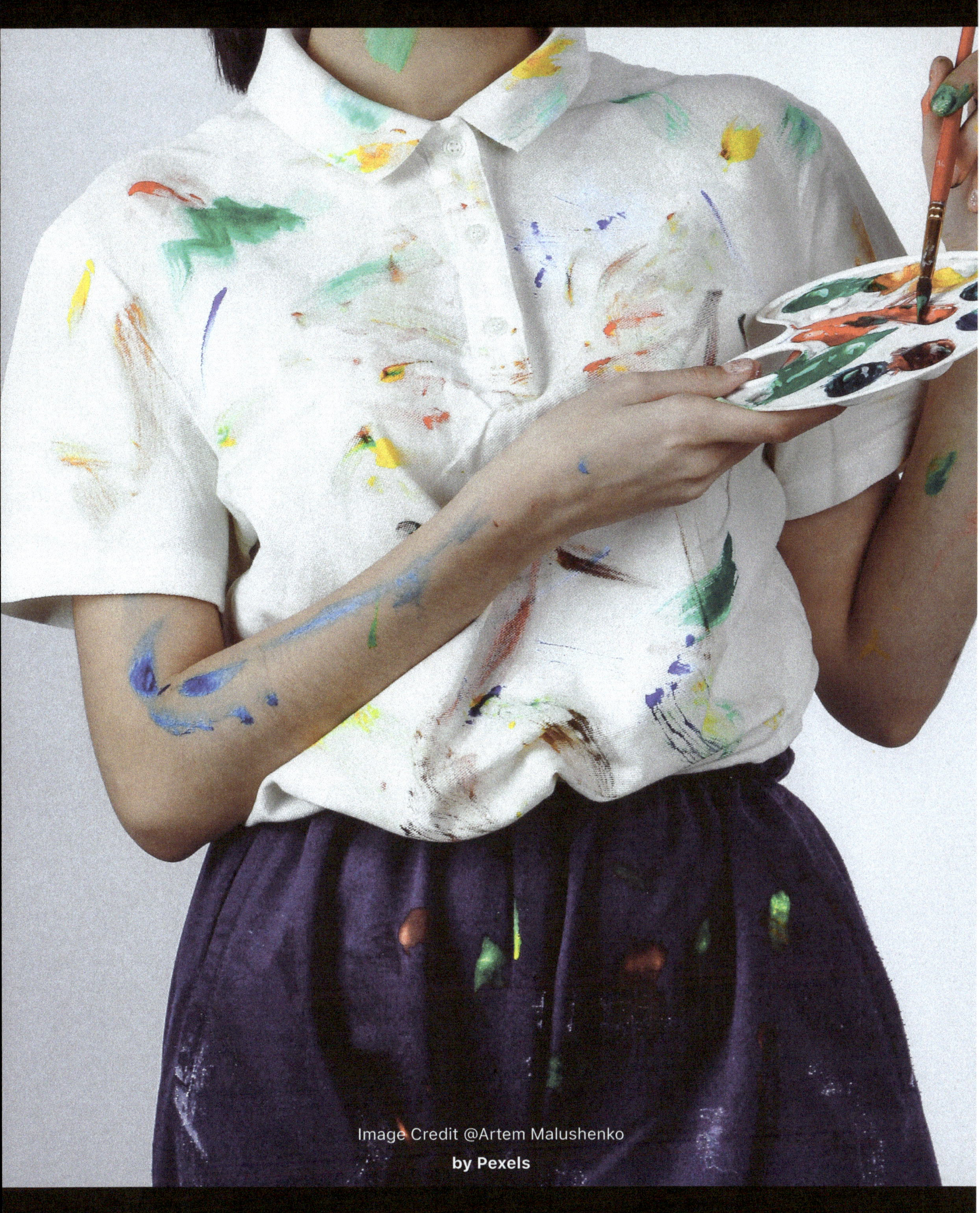
Image Credit @Artem Malushenko
by Pexels

What is an *Artist's* date?

Article by Volta Voloshin-Smith

As creatives and artists, it's important to spend time nurturing our creativity and going inward. It is equally as important to spend time in the world, collecting experiences that help shape us and our art. One way of doing just that is to go on Artist Dates.

The concept of Artists Dates comes from the iconic book The Artist Way by Julia Cameron. Personally, this book was what brought me back on the path of a creative life and career. The best part about this book is that you don't even need to complete it in its entirety to feel inspired and follow along with some of the prompts.

One of the practices that Julia Cameron advocates in her book is carving out time to do activities that nurture our creativity. Over the years, I've tried various Artist Dates activities and they always leave me full of creative energy and rejuvenation.

We also interviewed a few artists to hear about their favorite Artist Date activities:

"For my artist Dates I love to go or participate in a studio visit. But, having a meaningful conversation over a casual drink feels good too."

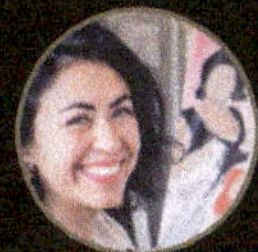

- PAULINA REE, OSLO, NORWAY
FIGURATIVE AND PORTRAIT ARTIST

There are a few requirements for an Artist Date:
It must ba a solo activity. Spending time with one self is a wonderful way to learn to appreciate the most important relationship we'll have in our lives. An artist date needs to last one to two hours. The more you can dedicate time, the better. An artist date is best when it's scheduled and on your calendar. We tend to give priorities to things that are on the calendar. So make yourself a weekly reminder! An artist date can't be a chore or an errand. It has to be a truly solo dedicated activity. It is preferred to do it once a week.

There are several benefits to having Artist Dates with yourself:
This is a great time to get clarity on a problem you're trying to solve Artist dates help you get out of your head by immersing yourself in a new activity Artists dates deepen creativity It's a great way to break from routine and get your brain a mental recharge. Artists dates are great for self care and self nurturing. Finally, Artist Dates can help increase self esteem. When we do activities for ourselves, keep the word to ourselves and show up, it increases our level of self respect and esteem. In order to cultivate esteem,we must do the actions that we regard in esteem.

"My idea of an artist date is Meeting in nature and painting in a public spaceI also love going to an Exhibition in this case."

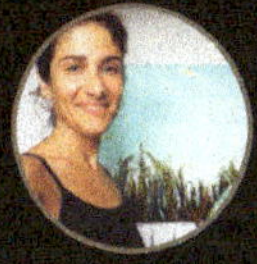

- CELIA SOTO, BRUSSELS
PAINTING, SINGING, DANCING ARTIST

"Living in South Korea for the past six years, For my artists dates I love going to museums and galleries to discover Korean artists. Day-trips to Seoul to visit the museums, galleries, and palaces are some of my most valued experiences here."

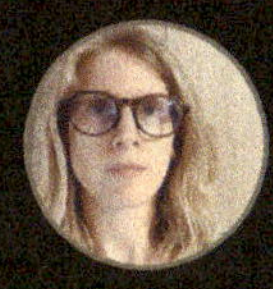

- SARA BACHER, SOUTH KOREA, USA
PAINTER

When looking for ideas for your Artist Date, ask yourself this question "What sounds fun and exciting?"
Follow that curiosity and find those activities that truly light you up. Here are a few ideas: Go to a farmers market and observe all the colors you can see Visit a nature trail and look for birds. Visit a local plant shop Watercolor a mandala. Attend a tea tasting. Tour a historic home in your area. Get up early and watch the sunrise from a tall building. Build something with legos.

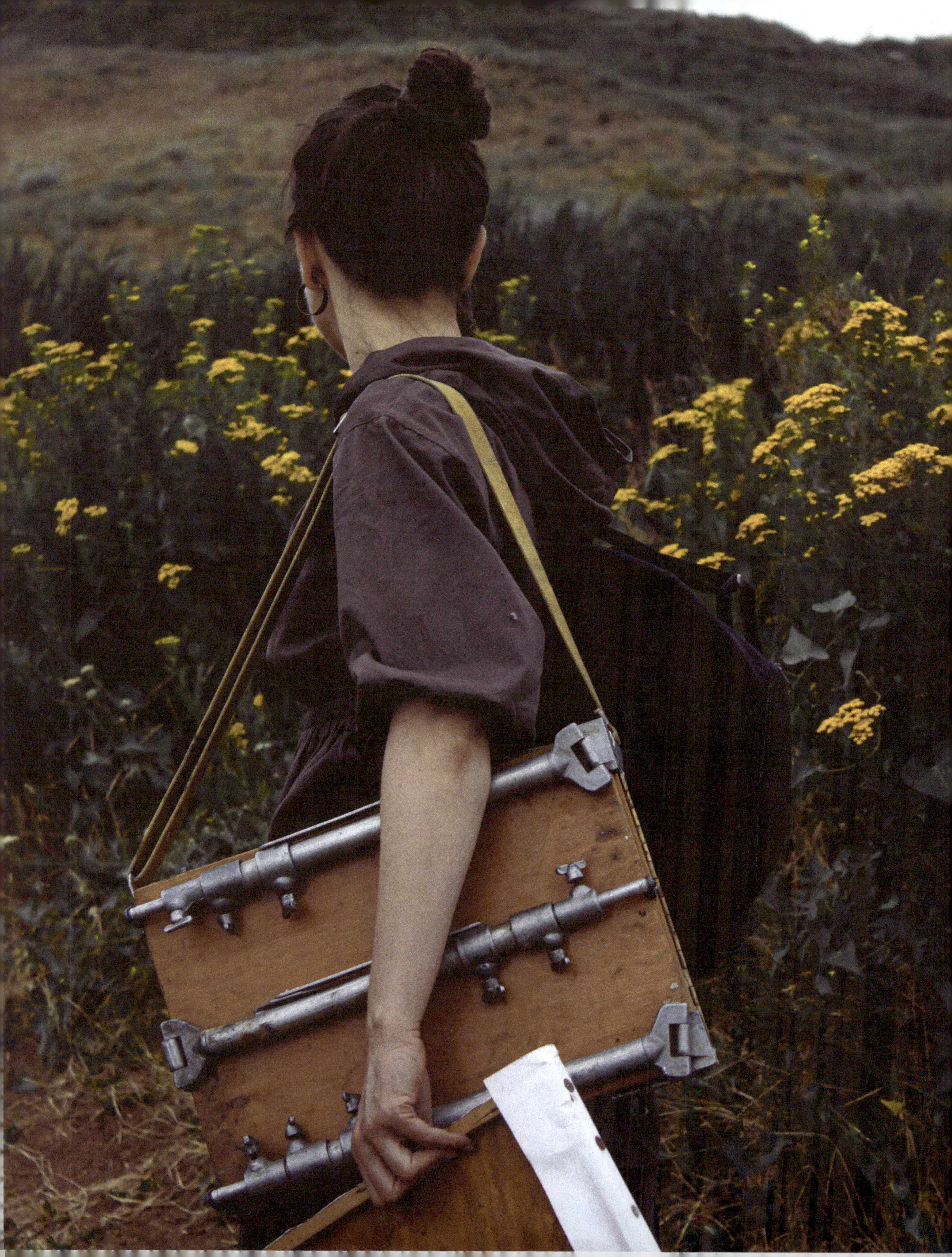

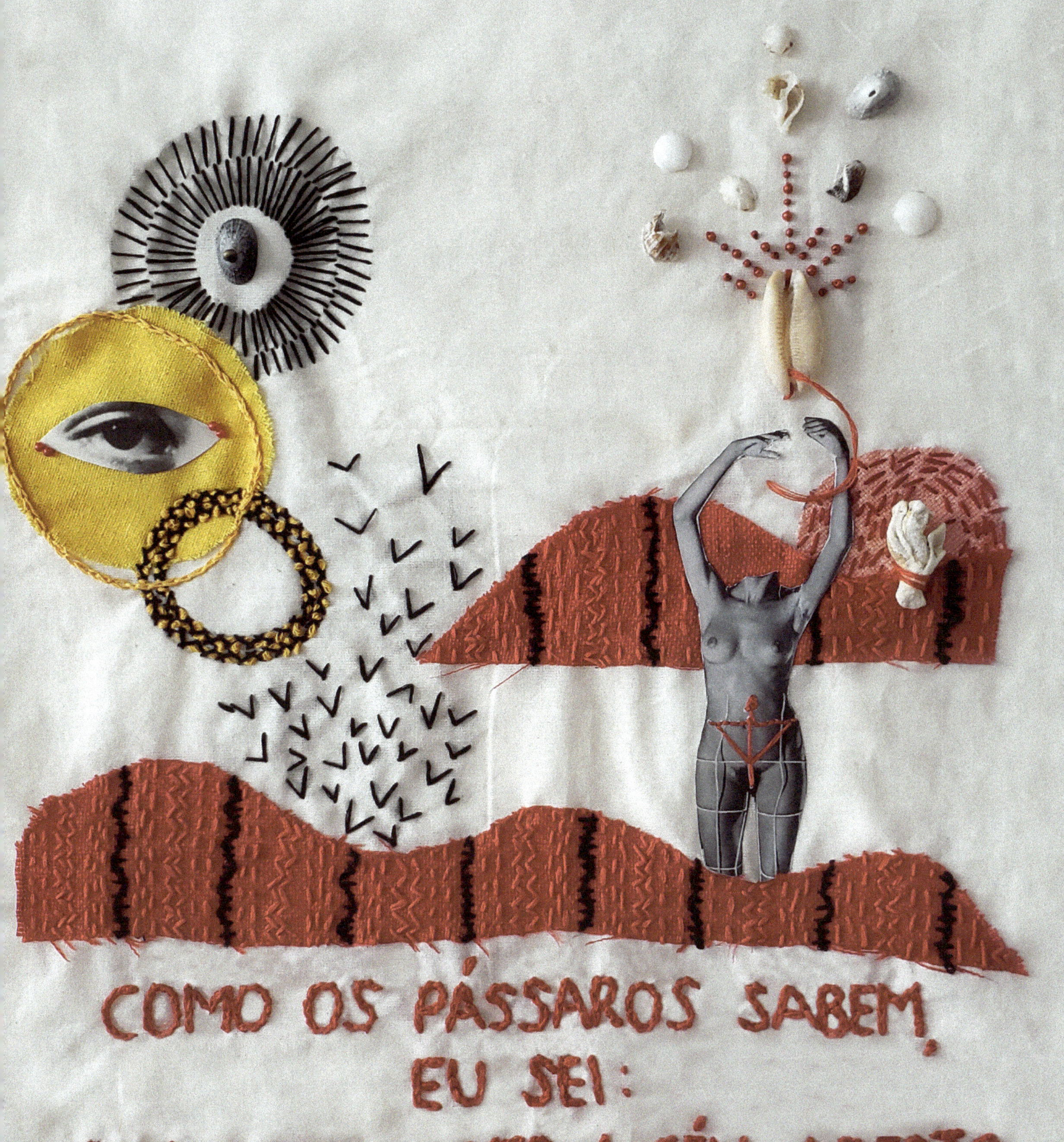

Image Credit @Heloísa Marques

Heloísa Marques on creating visual poems

Interview by Juliana Naufel

Heloísa Marques is a Brazilian Artist and Architect that dedicates her practice to creating visual poems using mixed media techniques such as collage and embroidery addressing the relationship between women, their bodies and the geographic space through which they circulate.

Can you tell us a little bit about yourself and your creative path?

I have been making collages since I was a child, before even knowing what it actually was or thinking about the use of this technique as a creative tool. I didn't create collages for many years, until one day I unsuspiciously decided to get back to it. There were these feelings that needed to be externalized, and making a collage seemed like a great way to do so. Collage is an accessible and democratic way of expression and as I perceive it, is a potent and disruptive technique that reframes and gives new meanings to fragments of photographs and other pre-existing artworks.

Crafts like embroidery, are very common practices among the women in my family. Since it was always associated as something the "gifted woman" should know, for a long time I didn't want to learn it, but somewhere along the way I felt that the collages weren't enough to communicate the stories I needed to tell through my work. I decided then that it could be interesting to merge these two techniques that, for long, were seen as "minor" forms of art, if compared to painting, for example.

I chose to subvert this manual technique that many times wasn't considered a legitimate knowledge– and that was used for centuries in a context of domesticating women and keeping them invisible between the boundaries of their homes, underneath the shadows of their handicraft work – to bring light upon other important questions, many of which are connected to the feminine, through the appreciation of the manual process itself.

What are the parallels between being an architect and an artist?

The main aspect of consonance between the two is my creative process, the way I elaborate what I create is vastly adapted from what I learned during my undergraduate studies. I create my artworks the same way I develop architectural works: I execute them always as a project, but the materials, execution and timelines change. One thing that keeps the same is the intention behind these works.

My Architecture Major is key when it comes to the concepts I choose to work with in my artistic practice. I have great interest for public and private spaces in which bodies commute – and even more so for the ones where they don't – and the reasons behind it. In a sense, I'm extremely inspired by the work of Beatriz Colombina, who explores, among other themes, the ones related to sexuality and space (as well as gender

> *"Collage is an accessible and democratic way of expression and as I perceive it, is a potent and disruptive technique that reframes and gives new meanings to fragments of photographs and other pre-existing artworks."*

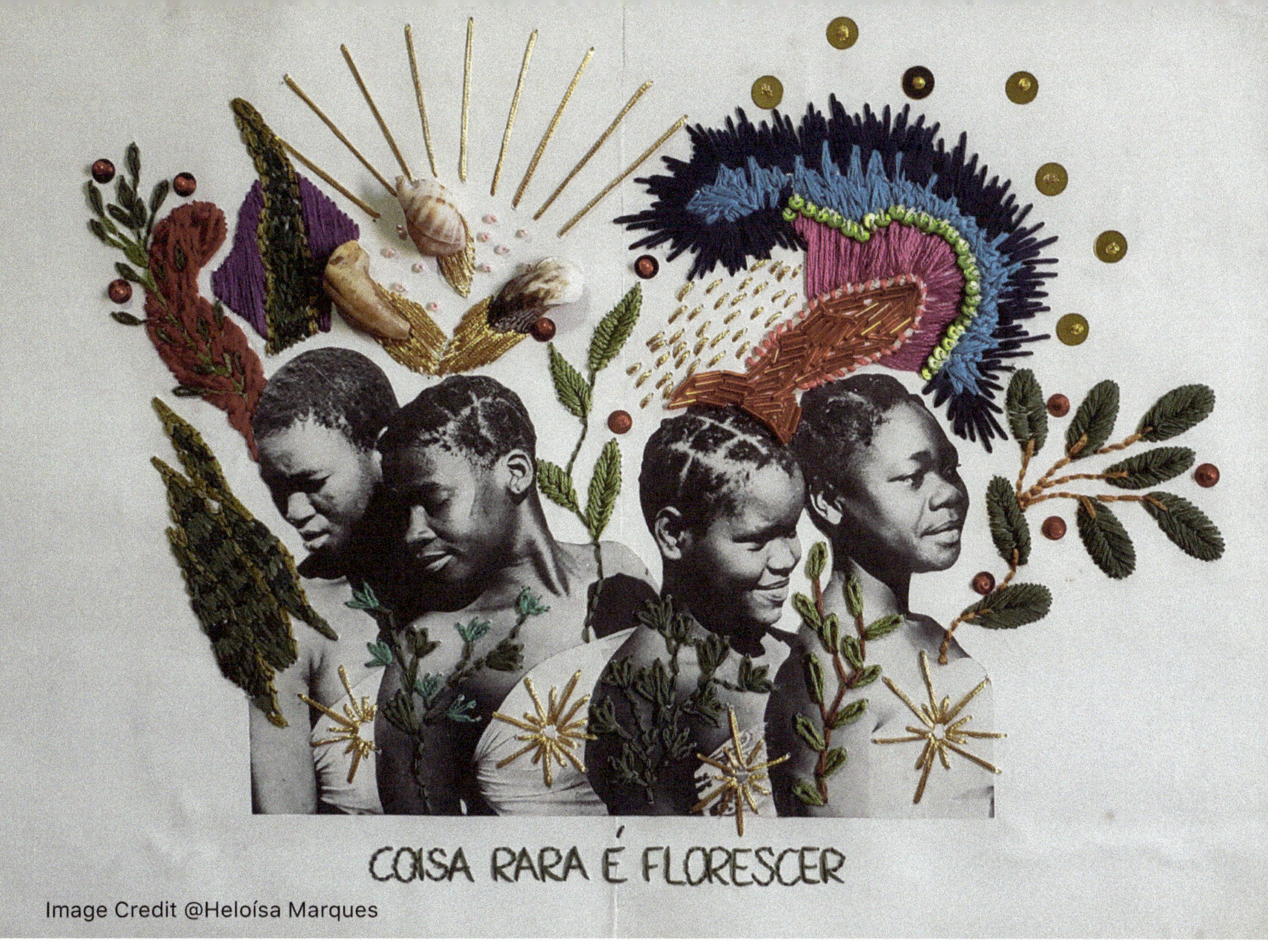

Image Credit @Heloísa Marques

Which other artists inspired you and showed you that there's a way of being an artist and making a living out of it?

My first inspiration of an artist that used the same technique as I do was you, Juliana Naufel. It is actually an honor for me to have become a reference for you as well and I'm grateful for all the exchanges and connections I made with other artists. Jess Vieira and Jamille Queiroz also inspire me quite a lot with their sensible truths and sensibilities. Their courage and discipline also inspire me to keep on creating.

What are your biggest challenges when it comes to being a woman artist in Brazil?

Brazil is facing an outrageous political and economic crisis and the setbacks can be seen in plain sight. As an artist that addresses gender-related themes, and someone who tries to communicate directly to women, I feel that we (artists or not) need to keep being attentive and fighting against the absurdity that has overthrown our daily lives. There is also a great amount of instability and depreciation about the arts, especially when it comes to techniques like textiles, which are still stigmatized and placed at a "lower" level than techniques such as painting, etc, so trying to earn a living from it is quite the challenge, but I keep doing it anyway.

When did you become interested in embroidery? What made you fall in love with the technique?

One day it occurred to me that letters and the processes that they go through (using your own handwriting, dispatching it, waiting for its arrival, reading something that was written days before) are being forgotten, replaced by faster and more instantaneous forms of communication. As I realized that, it made me feel anguished, so I decided to embroider sentences on my collages, like someone writes letters. That's why, at first, I only used paper - really old book covers that were 40 or 50 years old more specifically. Time passed by and I started to broaden the variety of supports I would use for my embroidery, which led me to work on larger pieces.

At first my works were made entirely as collages – even the embroidery – I would use fragments of other people's works, so my earliest writings were not my own. I like to reflect upon the power that the words carry, the way literature can be a source of inspiration for visual arts, and how it's possible to achieve new narratives using images that were already there.

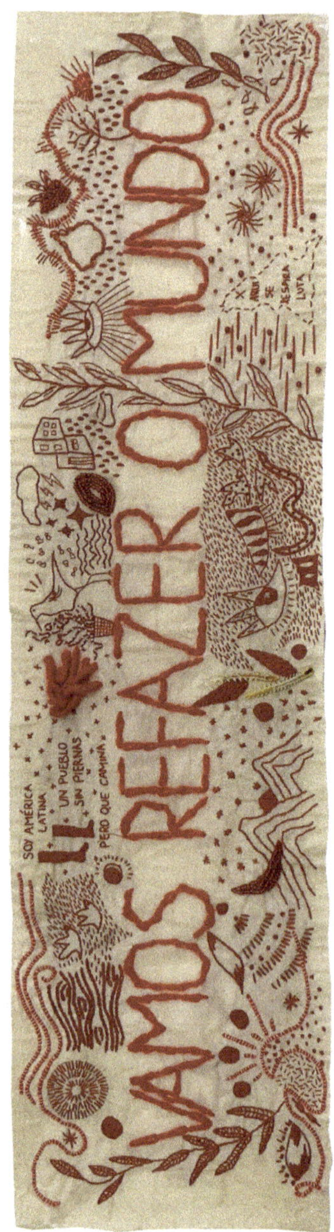

Image Credit @Heloísa Marques

"I like to reflect upon the power that the words carry, the way literature can be a source of inspiration for visual arts, and how it's possible to achieve new narratives using images that were already there."

A mix of different things guide me through this creative process: intuition, the sensible and unspeakable aspect of the images, the invisible potency of written things, and this knowledge that gains substance through the work of hands, beyond all the intrinsic complexity and multiplicity of the process itself.

Brazil is a stunning country with so many hidden gems! Can you tell us about the most beautiful place you've visited so far?
It has to be the Historic Center of Olinda! The town is listed as a World Heritage Site by UNESCO and it's one of the oldest towns in Brazil. Apart from its architectural beauty and its breathtaking views of the ocean, Olinda has a vibrant life and culture. It is home of the richest popular manifestations, like the best and greatest carnaval de rua in Brazil (yes, it is true), and there are many other festivities and local art studios open for visitation. I cannot recommend it highly enough.

Can you recommend us and describe one national dish that you think everyone should give it a try one day?
As a proud pernambucana (Brazilian citizen born in Pernambuco), I have a sweet tooth so I am really fond of sweets and desserts. I recommend locally made bolo-de-rolo, a type of cake that is recognized as a cultural and immaterial heritage of our state. Cartola is also very good, it's a dessert made with manteiga cheese (a local type of butter cheese) and fried bananas.

What brings you joy when you're not creating?
Going to the beach, cooking, traveling a lot, reading and going to parties.

Can you share a sweet memory related to your art practice?
Among the exhibitions, art fairs, galleries representing my work, creating commissioned works for international media outlets or embroidering a 1,00 x 1,40 m piece, the most meaningful moments are the connections I made with people. My social network increased vastly! Many opportunities happened because of these connections, but the greatest achievement is having found support and motivation to keep doing what I do, it's quite amazing.

What is one piece of advice you'd give to other creatives that are reading this?
I would tell them to follow their intuition. If you feel the urge to do something but think that you're not capable, try it a little bit more, be sensible about it and engage yourself. When it comes to being an artist, I'd say it's not about having a gift, it's all about the will you have of creating, the effort you put in your practice and being persistent.

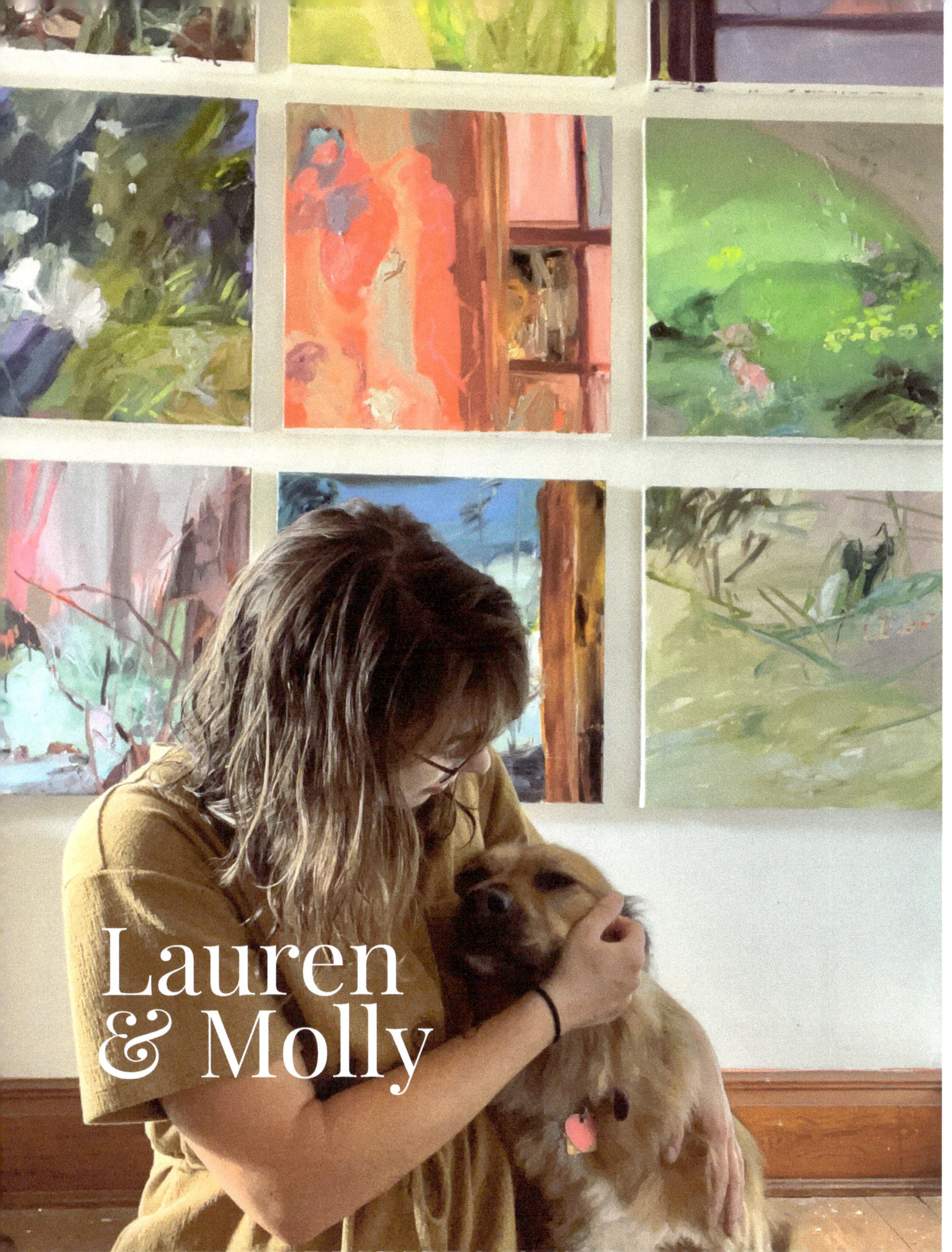
Lauren
& Molly

Meet THE STUDIO ASSISTANTS

Article by *Laurén Brady*

"Because of the dog's joyfulness, our own is increased. It is no small gift. It is not the least reason why we should honor as well as love the dog of our own life, and the dog down the street, and all the dogs not yet born. What would the world be like without music or rivers or the green and tender grass? What would this world be like without dogs?"

from Mary Oliver's "Dog Talk"

I believe Mary Oliver's words ring true to these creatures that bring us comfort, laughter, belonging to our creative processes and lives. I have a studio assistant named Molly. She's a 9-year-old rescued shepherd mix who has been lying below my easel for her entire life. She's had gesso dripped on her head, licked the tears off my face when I'm feeling overwhelmed by deadlines, and "danced"—hop-skipping and playfully yipping—along with me in the studio to music. Since Molly is such an underlying support in my studio, I wondered about other artists' studio assistants. I had the pleasure of talking with a few artists about their own companions. Here are some of their stories:

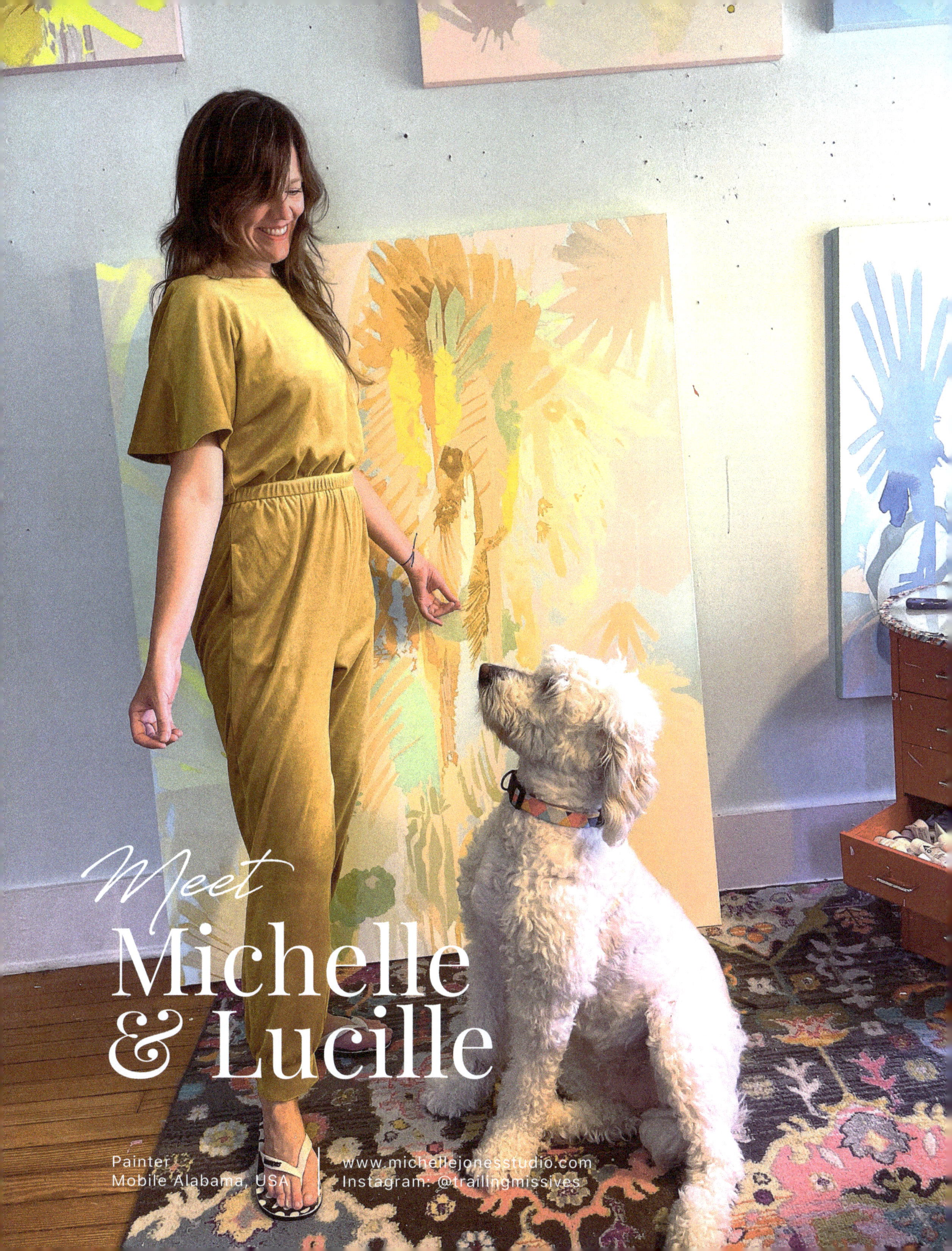

Meet
Michelle
& Lucille
Painter
Mobile Alabama, USA
www.michellejonesstudio.com
Instagram: @trailingmissives

The Time Keeper

"Lucille knows our routine really well.
After riding in the car to drop off my daughter at school,
she goes upstairs and waits for me at the studio door."

Interview by *Laurén Brady*

Michelle Jones has always had studio pets. When her daughter was one, they welcomed Lucille, the goldendoodle puppy, to their family. Michelle laughed that while they had this new toddling creature, they also had Lucille running around the house. Lucille quickly became accustomed to the daily schedules of her family. She is almost always by Michelle's side, especially in the studio hanging out among the canvas-filled space. At one point while answering a question, Lucille put her head on Michelle's lap and looked up as if supporting what her mom was saying.

"She knows our routine really well. After riding in the car to drop off my daughter at school, she goes upstairs and waits for me at the studio door. Sometimes if I take too long listening to a podcast or making eggs, she almost shames me when I get to my studio... as if I am making her late." Lucille loves to lay under the table, prominently in front of the painting that Michelle was planning to work on, or the far side of the studio so that she can keep watch out the window. Michelle recalled working on a series of paintings that had a pale color palette when Lucille dipped her tail in black paint and started wagging her tail and slinging paint around. Somehow, no paint landed on the new work!

Lucille is a quiet, steady presence. When asked what is the best part of having a pet as a studio assistant, Michelle responded, "She's a good timekeeper. A reminder of the fullness and reality of life, even outside of this space, helping me know when it's time to check out for the day. She gently tells me by standing up and stretching." She is always present, and this helps Michelle be the same.

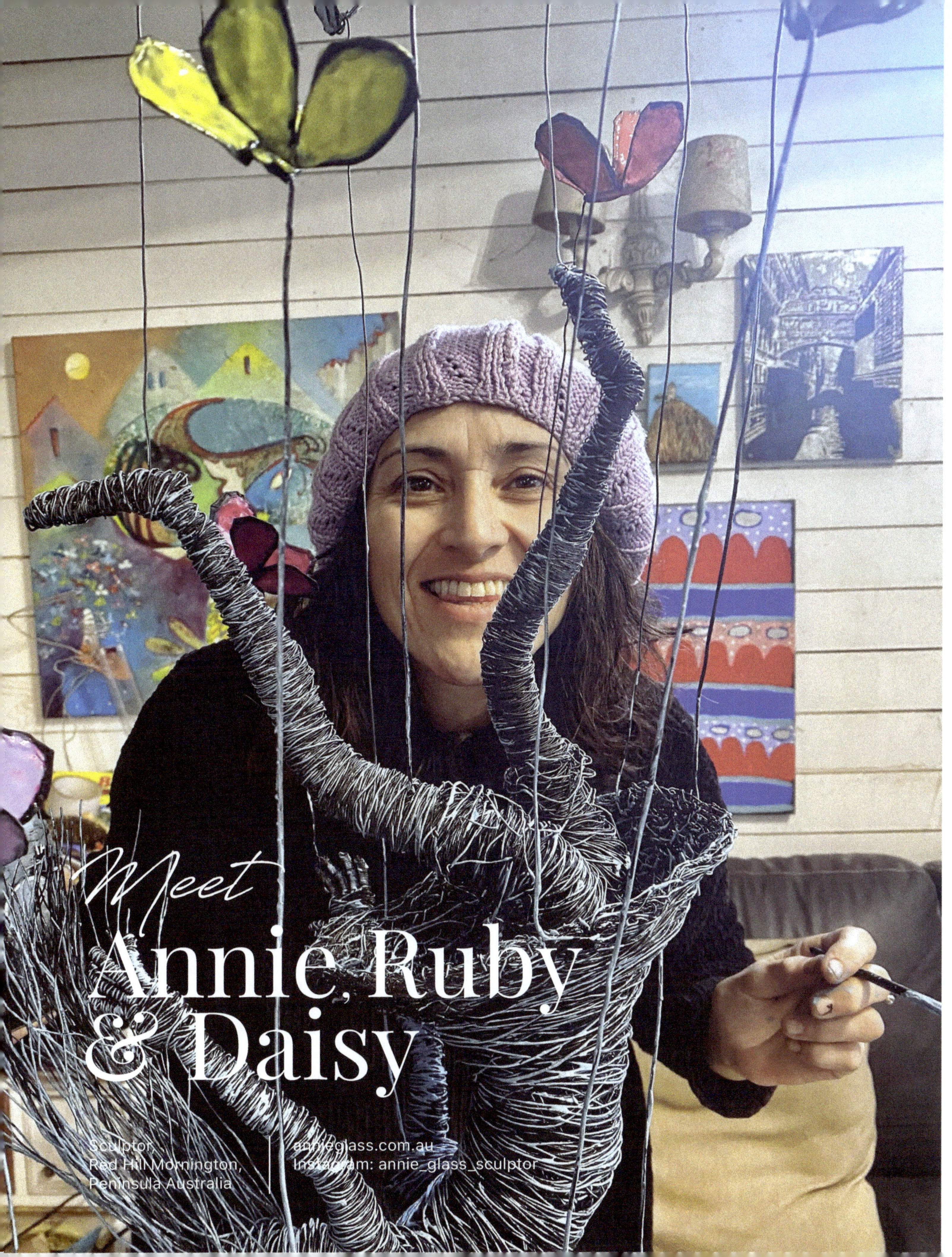

Meet
Annie, Ruby
& Daisy
Sculptor
Red Hill Mornington,
Peninsula Australia
annieglass.com.au
Instagram: annie_glass_sculptor

The Inspiration of a Sculptor

"Sometimes it's a lonely existence [as an artist], and my animals comfort me. I adore them, she said, tearing up. She feels grateful to be able to work long hours in her studio with the company of her animals."

Interview by *Laurén Brady*

Annie lives in the country with her chickens, a horse, and two dogs. Ruby is a five year-old great dane cross who is a gentle giant, and Daisy is a sweet, adorable, and intelligent seven-month old goldendoodle. The pups' daily routine involves lying on their beds in the studio and watching Annie work, taking walk breaks, visiting the chickens, and working again. Daisy is best friends with their horse, Stewie, a rescued ex-racehorse. One of Annie's favorite memories is Stewie walking into her studio and looking at artwork. Imagine a beautiful brown horse strolling through a room packed with finished and in-process work, supplies, books. He moved carefully taking in the scenery but being watchful of each step. Stewie has sipped Annie's coffee and sometimes looks for snacks—he's very much at home in the studio.

The deep connection Annie has with her animals is clear in the way they inspire her art where movement and observation of daily life are main themes. She spoke of the challenge of referencing specific breeds of dogs and finding ways to manipulate the materials to convey different textures of fur. Because of this, she most often references Ruby and other crossbreeds. In older works, Annie created bronze sculptures—one particular piece showed a dog caught mid-roll on its back. Her current work involves kinetic wire sculpture. Shake is created with wire and glass beads that capture water flying off a dog as it shakes. The swirling beads and subtle wiggles of the steel wire suggest the joy and silliness of an ordinary occurrence in the life of a dog and the strength of the relationship with humans.

Sometimes it's a lonely existence [as an artist], and my animals comfort me. I adore them, she said, tearing up. She feels grateful to be able to work long hours in her studio with the company of her animals. They are her muses, her companions, a reason she loves what she does so much.

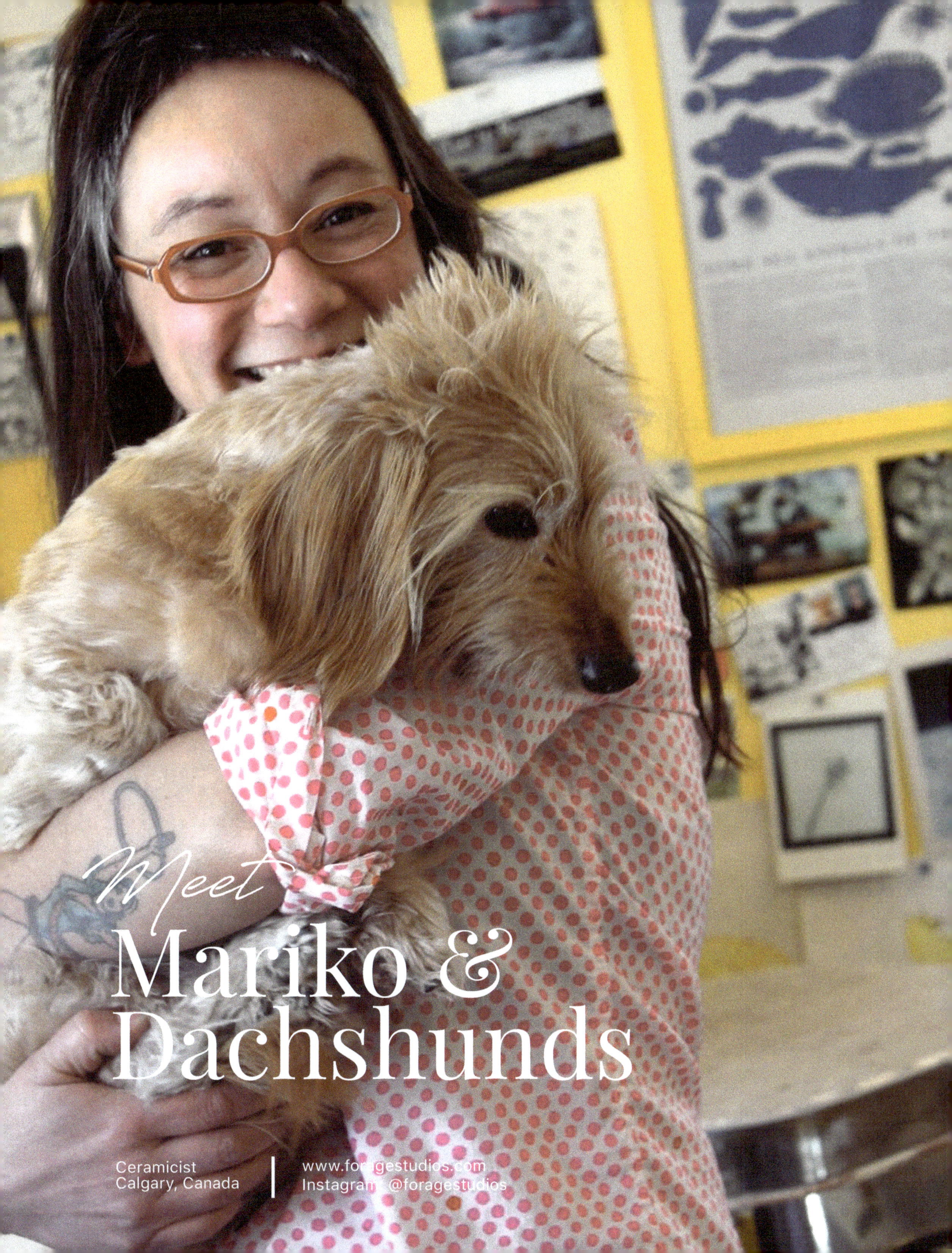

Meet
Mariko &
Dachshunds
Ceramicist
Calgary, Canada
www.foragestudios.com
Instagram: @foragestudios

The Playful Spirit

"We would push all the canvassed studio tables together and the dogs (Mr. Pickles and Angus at the time) and the students would use their accumulated skills to model the dogs."

Interview by *Laurén Brady*

Mariko Paterson's love of dachshunds began in an undergraduate art history class when a slide of Giacomo Balla's work, Dynamism of a Dog on a Leash was projected. She said, "The first time I laid eyes on the piece, I somehow knew they would be fun and be total characters." At one time she had four dachshunds—RIP Rodney, Mr. Pickles, and Angus. If you follow Mariko on social media, you'll be familiar with the sweet faces of two long haired dachshunds, Mr. Tubes and Bernard.

Mr. Tubes and Bernard are best frien ds and are never far from Mariko. In her studio their favorite spot is under her main work table where they lay on their beds burrowed in blankets. Their unofficial task is to be "Nature's Broom"—collecting dust or tape from packing and shipping pieces. The pups remind Mariko to take breaks as she often becomes too engrossed in her process to pause. If she tries to work past 5:00 pm, the dogs' fidgeting signals that it's time to quit. Mariko taught at the Alberta College of Art and Design, now called UAARTS, and shared a memory of bringing in her dogs to model in her ceramic classes. She said,

"We would push all the canvassed studio tables together and the dogs (Mr. Pickles and Angus at the time) and the students would use their accumulated skills to model the dogs. It was a completely disarming experience for the models and the students alike, and it was amazing to see what they, the students, could accomplish in such a short time. Of course the dogs were in it for the pets, but their presence somehow alleviated the pressure on the students to "perform" or make something "good." I don't think any student ever got less than a joyous grade of A for this project and the dogs' energy was completely infectious."

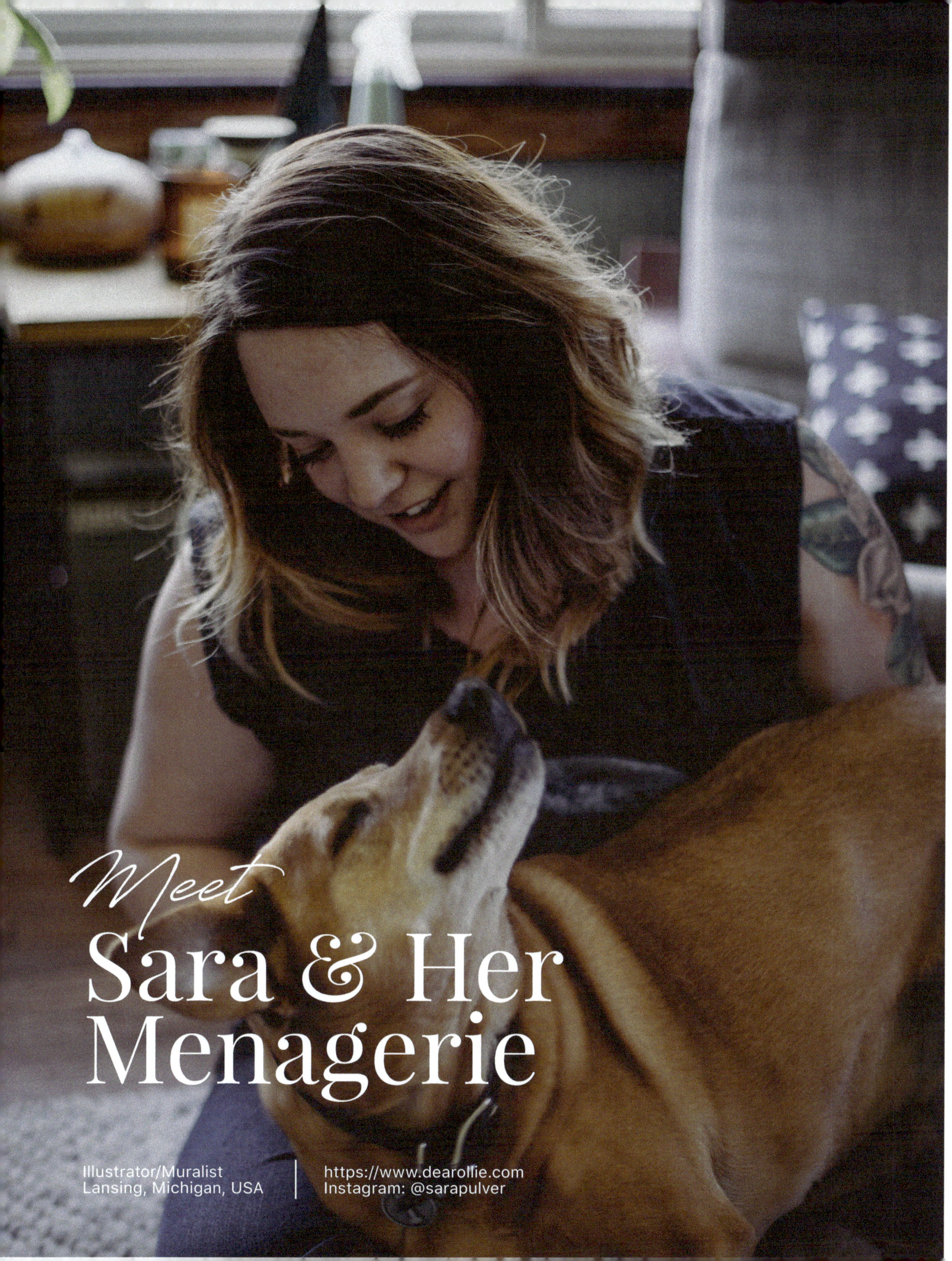

Meet
Sara & Her Menagerie

Illustrator/Muralist
Lansing, Michigan, USA

https://www.dearollie.com
Instagram: @sarapulver

Pulver's Menagerie

"The dogs were immediately by her side – Reid made sure that he was in Sara's sight while Ollie leaned against her. Like they were saying, we've been here before. We will be okay."

Interview by *Laurén Brady*

Sara Pulver is an illustrator and muralist whose assistants include two dogs, Reid and Ollie, two cats, Cosmo and Scribbles, and five chickens. Her day starts by taking care of the animals—feeding, watering, walking—then making coffee and settling into her work. As she draws, Cosmo likes to chase Sara's Apple Pen, as evidenced by the tiny teeth marks at the top. He also enjoys rolling on her laptop—and yes, he has deleted a few files! When Sara works outdoors the chicken noises and scratches make an entertaining backdrop. Most days, though, Sara creates inside with the two dogs at her feet.

In 2014 Sara founded Dear Ollie, a line of illustrated paper goods and gifts named after Oliver, the pitbull cattle dog mix. Her business, like the pup, is a bit snarky but also sweet and uplifting. Observing her pets has vastly influenced her illustrations. "Generally my subject matter is some sort of animal with a pun or phrase alongside it. The animals definitely infuse their personalities into the work." One of her first sticker designs was a cat hissing the word "No".

Sara recalled a memory from early in her career when preparing for markets and fairs caused anxiety. Feeling overwhelmed and sensing a panic attack beginning, she would sit on the floor to catch her breath. The dogs were immediately by her side – Reid made sure that he was in Sara's sight while Ollie leaned against her. Like they were saying, "we've been here before. We will be okay."

Studio pets provide unrelenting companionship and joy; they're completely ingrained into the day. Sara said, "As someone who has struggled with mental health issues, they're always a reason to get up. I have to water the chickens or walk the dogs. It can feel so much more difficult to take care of ourselves, but it's always rewarding taking care of them, and by doing that, that's taking care of yourself."

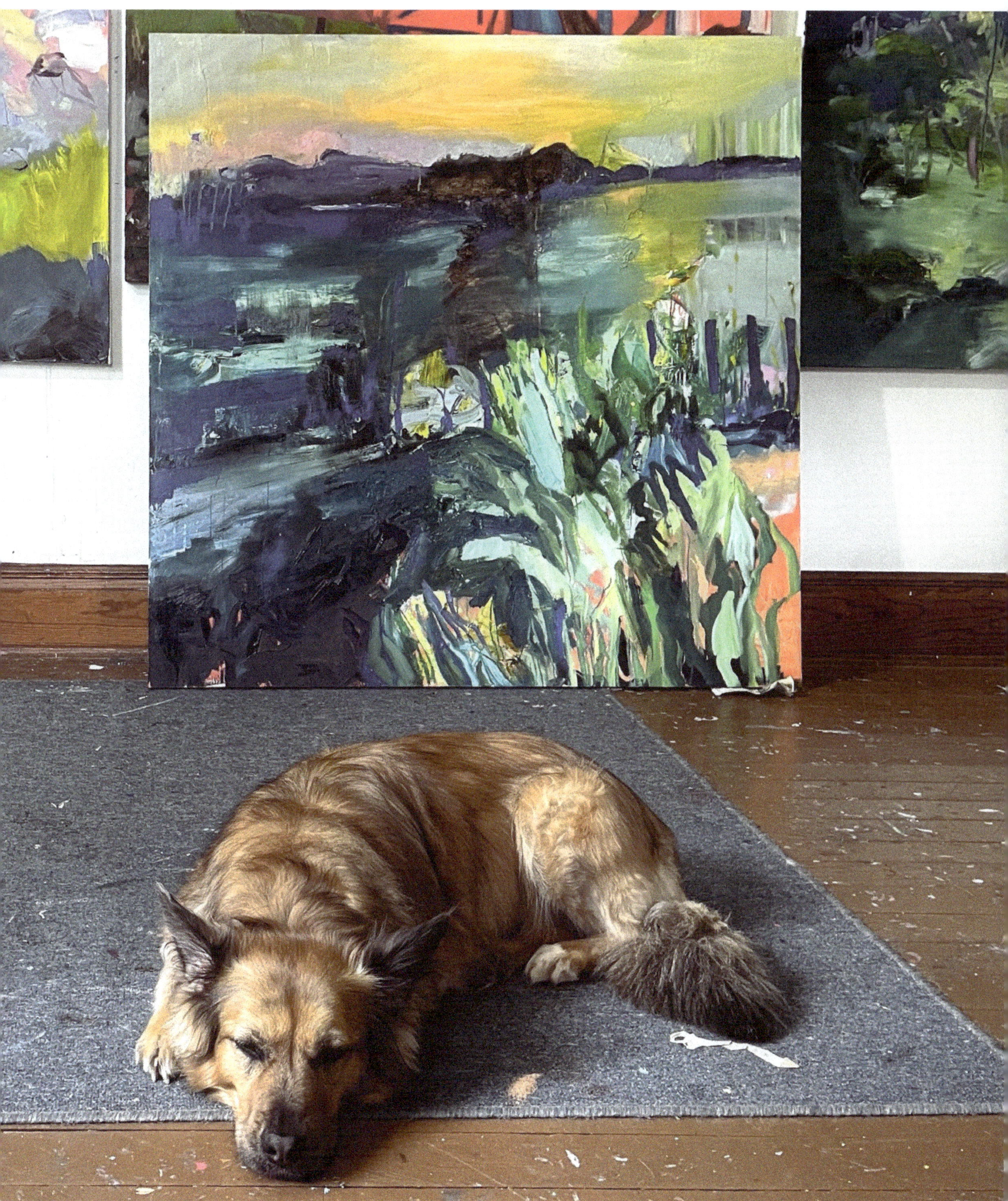

From my conversations with these artists and from my own experience, it's clear that studio pets work their way into the heart of our creative practices. Their presence provides support, sheer goofiness, unwavering companionship, and inspiration. They remind us, in their own ways, that it's okay to take breaks and to be present. As I write this, I am in my studio, and Molly is lying at my feet. I know that once I move to paint, she will be there, under my easel, ready to get to work.

To see my paintings (and photos of Molly assisting), you can find me on Instagram *@laurenbradyart* or my website *www.laurenbradyart.com*. I'd love to hear about your studio pets too!

The worst advice you have recieved

ARTIST EDITION

Article by *Rabia Khan*

In this life, we'll all come across individuals offering sound advice or lashing out at us with hurtful words. But our reaction to it is entirely up to us. When we asked the ATH community members for the worst advice they had ever received as an artist, We were astounded by the responses we got. So keep reading because we have included some of them in this article.

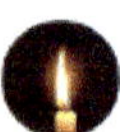

evasolisarte Join every possible art exhibition and/or contest. It meant to keep creating to fit in, got a bit lost, busy letting all those go.

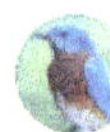

absolute_nobodies_art Draw faster. Which in some cases is valuable but in a finished work speed over quality is NOT ideal

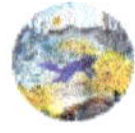

maaikedrawingsandjewelry When I was in primary school I was told to 'draw between the lines' all the time..

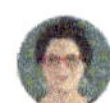

design_susekopp I wanted to study costume design after school. I showed my work to the professor in charge and he told me I should never think of studying anything creative. Biology would be better for me. Makes me still angry today! And guess what? Earning my living with graphic design since more than 20 years.

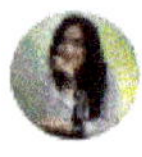

artbygissele "Consider changing your art style so you may be included in our gallery."

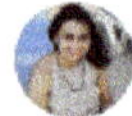

pallavi_art_ U need to make you art more "sellable" so change ur art to what sells in the market

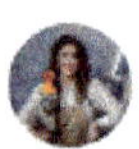

lafolkner You need a stable job to have security. (I'm booked til next June)

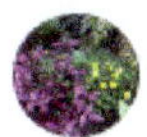

sophiachommy Why paint just women 😄😄

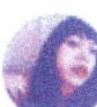

dreamlovemelody @maaikedrawingsandjewelry my dad used to say that to me ALL the time and for that reason I keep all my work to myself in my studio 😣 I was always so annoyed but I also learned why it was important to seek out support from other creative connections

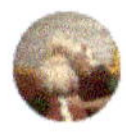

carolefreehealy Not words, but a teacher who painted on my painting for about 5 minutes and then said "like that!" I have no idea what she was trying to show me... Except my painting was ruined.

dgardner1463 It's great using your imagination but what happens when you get older and no longer have it? My A level Art Teacher. I'm definitely older and definitely still imagining ❤️

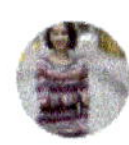

anais_are @carolefreehealy That's horrible. Reminds me of a the time an art teacher cut one of the legs off my figureskater sculpture. The supporting leg, I might ad. She said "it was just hanging there". 😟

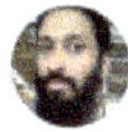

sukesankanka Use grey color and don't make details in your. That's why people are not buying 😟(A COMMENT FROM THE PEOPLE)

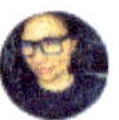

simonehesterart You'll never make any money.
Granted, I'm by no means financially rich, but I'm rich in my heart and soul because I choose to follow my passion. I wouldn't trade that for anything.

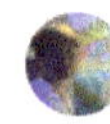

carinaearlart @sukesankanka omg I have received the exact same advice!!!! It's bs. I muted my tones so much in school bc of this advice and even used grey which I didn't like. Those pieces have never sold. But my newer pieces full of color and you ambiguous details are very popular and are my bread

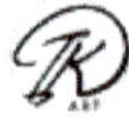

irene_k_art "A known artist told me: "You'll never get into the art institute". A year later i got in!

thebodylovealchemist To not paint larger works because they are too hard to sell and average people don't have the space to buy or sell them.

Don't spend time painting pieces when you don't make at least 75,000 dollars so you can be supported.

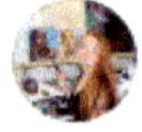

ellatakerart Two I still get to this "Art is not a valid career / Art won't pay the bills" & "People don't like that much color on their walls, try painting neutrals and more decorative art"

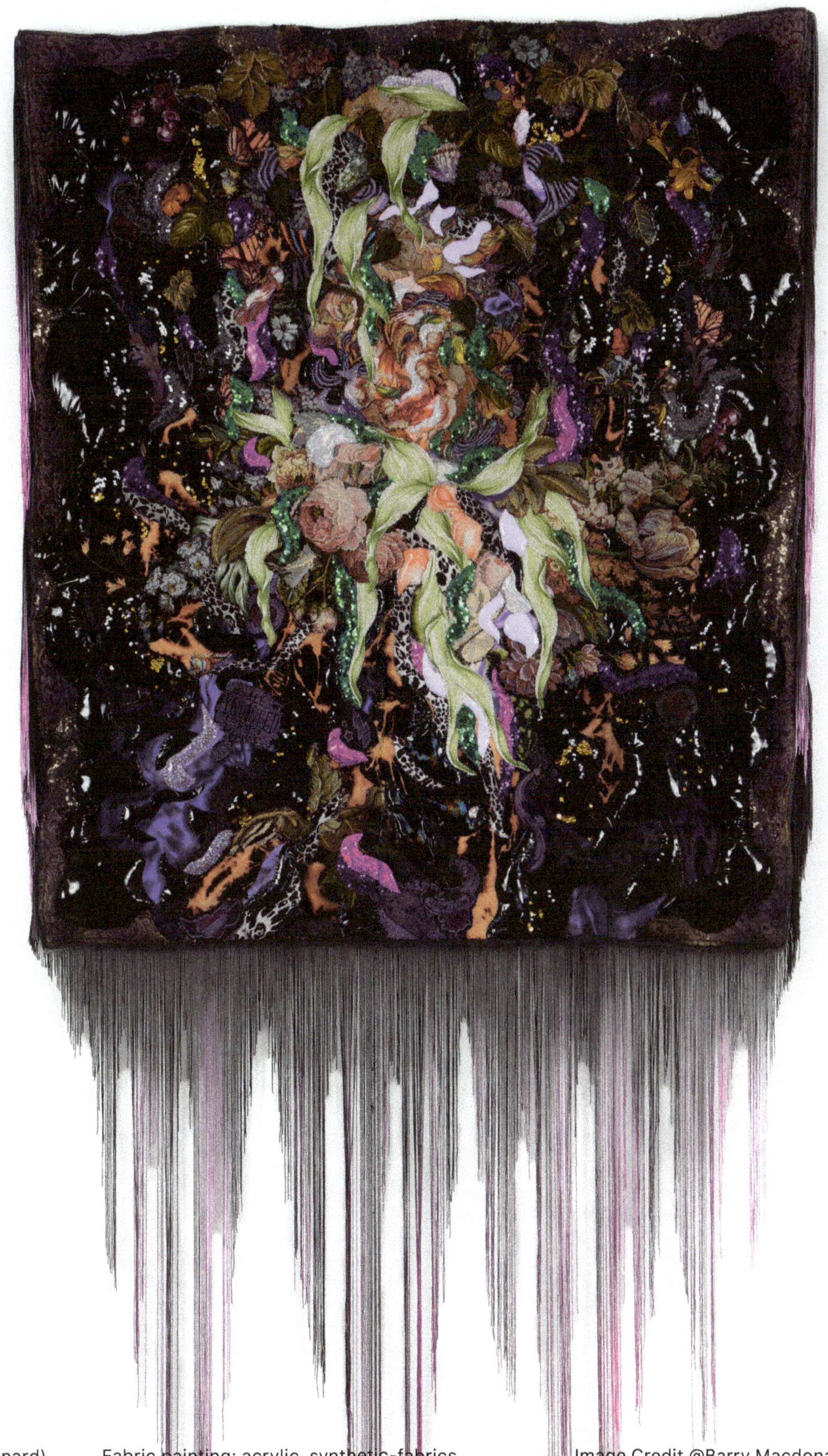

Untitled (After Fragonard)
105 x 170 cm
2021

Part of Private Collection,
The Netherlands

Fabric painting: acrylic, synthetic-fabrics,
sequin fabric, tapestry-fabric, hand-
embroidery, polyester wadding, and hand-
dyed tassel fringes on canvas.

Image Credit @Barry Macdonald

48

Curated Artists

Learn all about the work, process, and inspiration of the curated artists from all around the world by digging into their creative careers.

Emily Mullet
Catlin Catwright
Malin Gyllensvaan
Sarah Detweiler
Joanna Pilarczyk
Leah Guzman
Rachel Le Roux

Fatemha Ibrahim
Elisa Vita
Sydney Herndon
Ana Sneeringer
Shivanghi Ladha
Anne Von Freyburg
Karen Turner

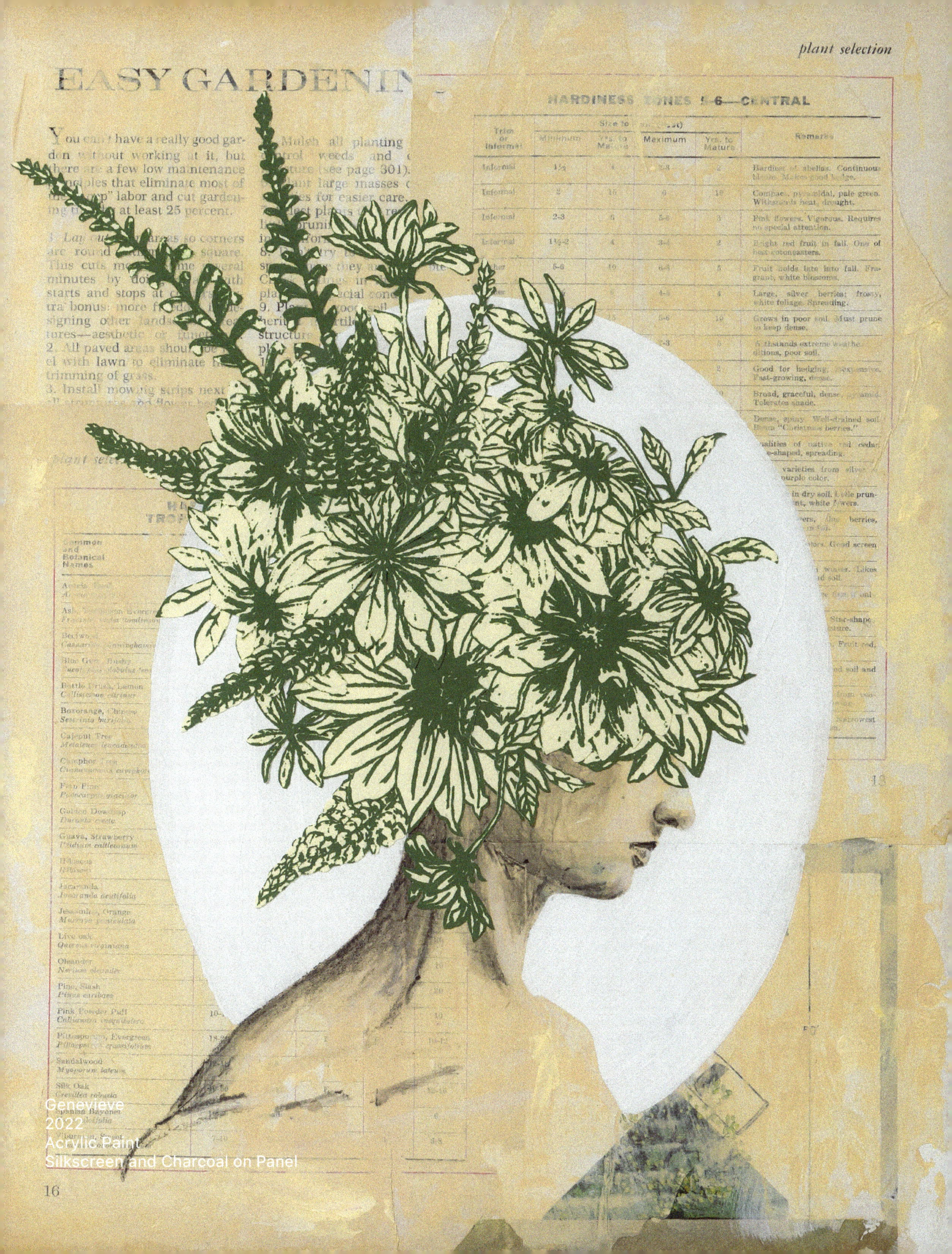

Genevieve
2022
Acrylic Paint
Silkscreen and Charcoal on Panel

16

Emily Mullet

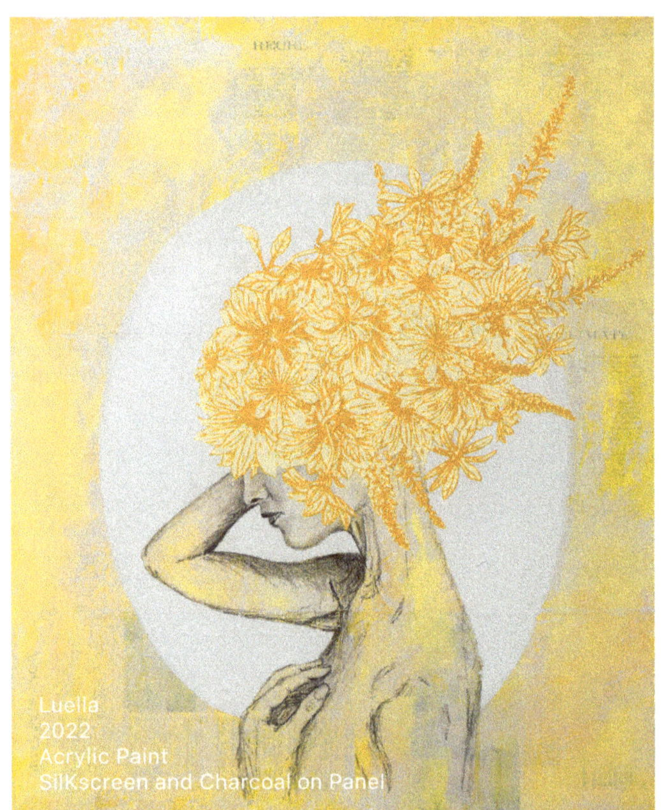

A *mixed media artist*
Based in Pennsylvania, USA.
She uses *printmaking* Techniques to
explore her Interest in *floral imagery*
And the *female form*.

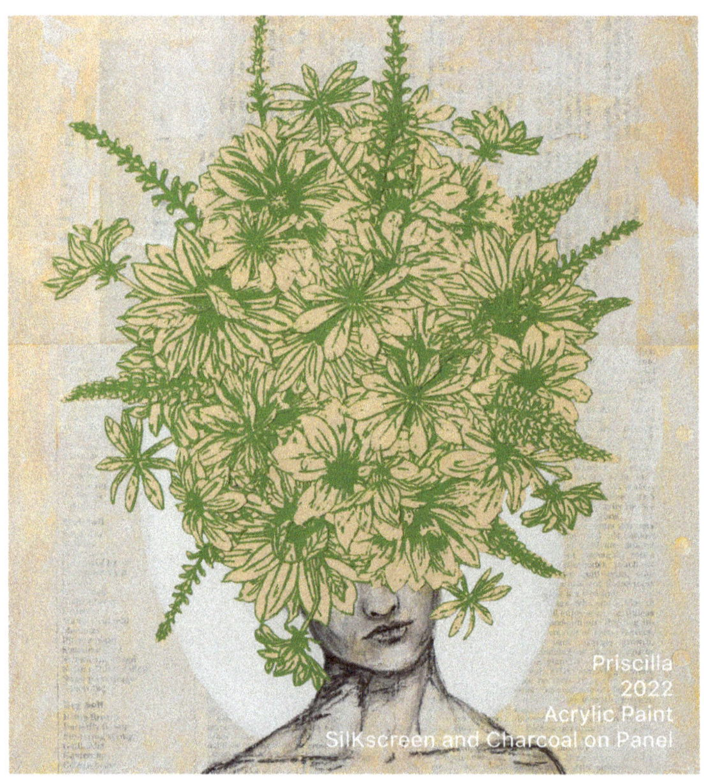

https://www.emilymullet.com/

 @emilymullet

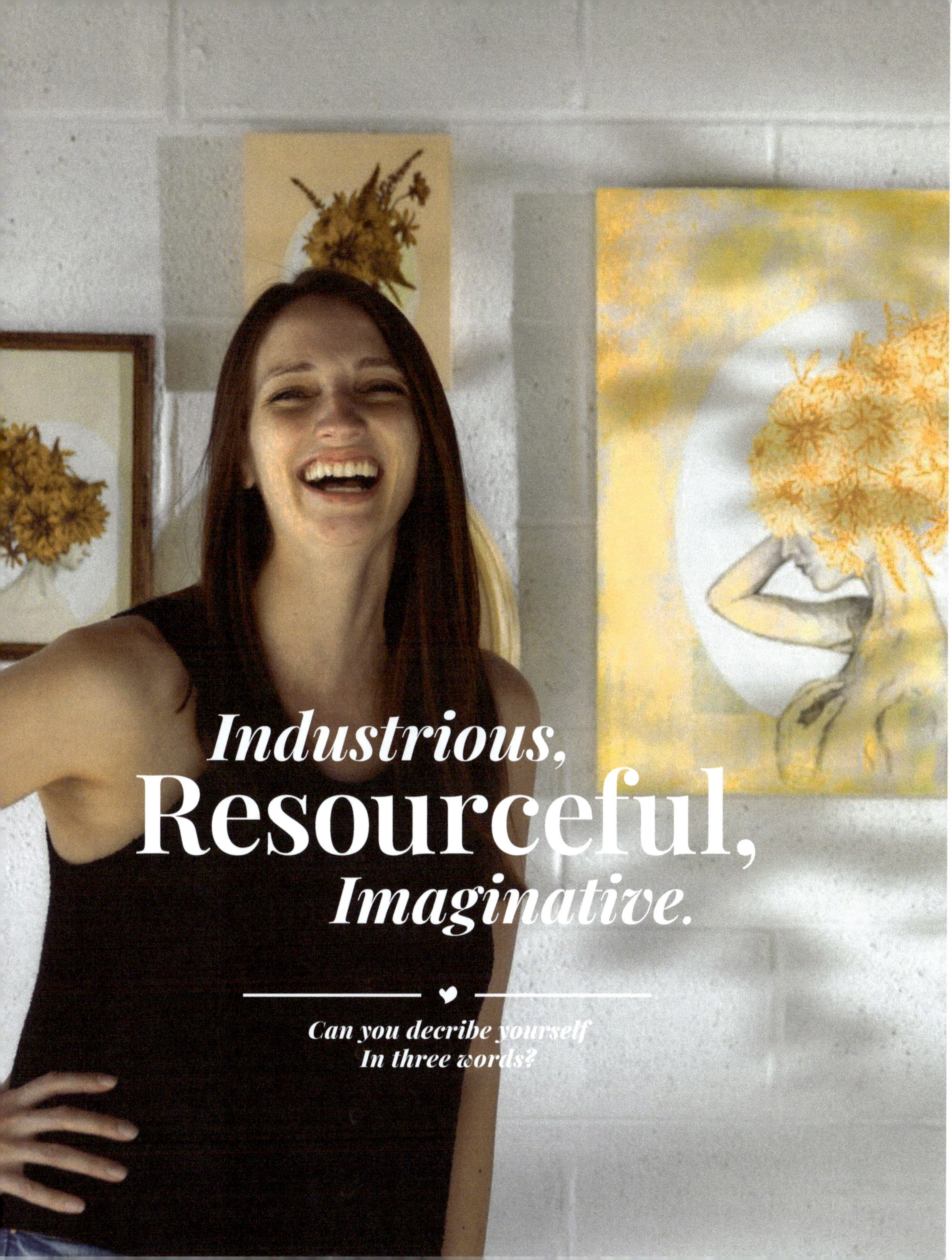

Industrious,
Resourceful,
Imaginative.

Can you decribe yourself
In three words?

"My motto for years has been to prioritize people."

Emily received a Bachelor of Arts in Studio Art with an emphasis in Painting and Graphic Design from College of the Ozarks in 2012. Much of Emily's work is influenced by contemporary street artists, drawing inspiration from aerosol paints, stencils, and wheat pastes. Emily completed an apprenticeship at Moravian Ahas been featured by PxP Contemporary, Arts to Hearts Project, SHOWFIELDS, and CandyFloss Magazine.

In her most recent collection, Mind Blooms, Emily collages silkscreened florals to create female portraits. These portraits explore the idea of the mind as a vast garden.

SO, TELL US ABOUT THE WORK YOU MAKE & WHY?

My body of work, Mind Blooms, is by far the most personal art collection I've created. I feel as though it has been years in the making and is now finally manifesting itself. The series explores the idea of the mind as a vast garden. In tending to your mind, one can prune, trim, and transplant to meet the expectations of a well-maintained garden. The priority of this method is to blend in or match what your fellow gardeners are cultivating. However, the artist's mind, featured in these portraits, prioritizes a different method. It is a method that seeks to value the native plants of the mind—personal traits and strengths. The goal of this gardener is to nurture the nuances of one's mind instead of replacing them. It's here the garden evolves into something more beautiful and wild than any preplanned garden.

To create the collection, Each portrait is titled with a female name, also from the Victorian era. The flowers used in these portraits are lupine (imagination and possible portal to the fairy world), acanthus (the fine arts), and dahlias (elegance, inner strength, and change.

WHERE DO YOU FIND YOUR PURPOSE AS AN ARTIST?

First and foremost, I am the healthiest and most content version of myself when creating. It is truly therapy for my soul. If I do not allow myself the space to create, I, as well as those around me, suffer. Therefore, my purpose as an artist is to fully embrace the joy and exploration of creativity. This embrace is an act of self-love.

My secondary purpose as an artist is more others-centered. My art practice includes being open with my process of creating art, making conceptual discoveries, and even sharing failed experiments. This can feel intrusive for some artists, but it's the opposite for me. I feel absolutely energized when revealing these parts of my studio practice. By continually allowing others to observe my growth and exploration, individuals following my work are invited on the same journey. My self-discoveries become their self-discoveries. The freedom I find to learn from mistakes is extended to those watching. Confidently speaking about my work emboldens others to do the same. Whenever someone reaches out to me and shares how my journey has encouraged them, I know I am on the right path.

WHAT WOULD YOU DO WITH YOUR ART, IF YOU HAD NO FEAR?

If I had no fear, I would pursue creating public works of art. I find large murals and public installations incredibly inspiring and important for the community. However, I am intimidated by their permanence! I enjoy seeing how my artwork evolves and matures over time. The thought of having a previous version of myself on display makes me nervous. Maybe one day I will work up the courage to conquer this fear

IF YOU HAVE THE WORLD'S ATTENTION FOR 30 SECONDS, WHAT IS THAT YOU WOULD LIKE TO SAY?

My motto for years has been "prioritize people." I am someone who can easily get lost in my career or my world of creativity. Without even realizing it, I often ignore those around me. But prioritizing meaningful relationships with others is far more precious than anything I can create.

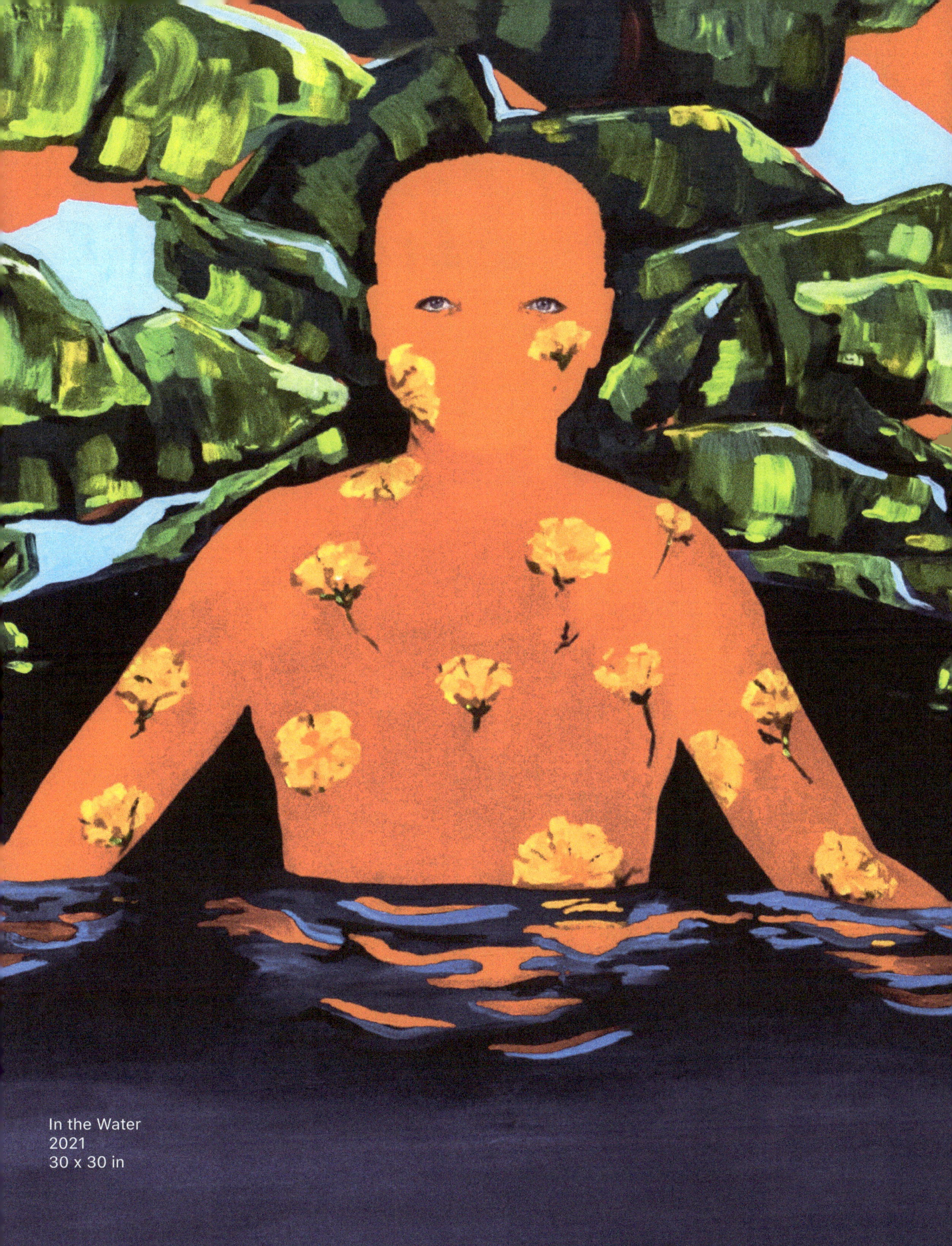

In the Water
2021
30 x 30 in

Caitlin Catwright

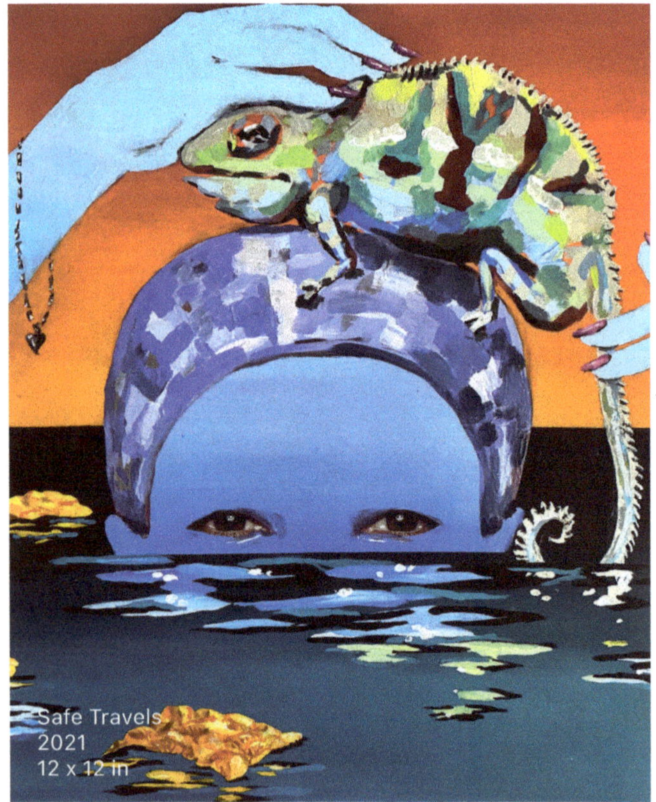

www.caitlincartwright.com

[Instagram] @caitlincatwright

A Detroit-based *social change artist* whose vibrant narrative works combine *painting, drawing, and collage* to explore the stories that connect people across cultures and circumstance.

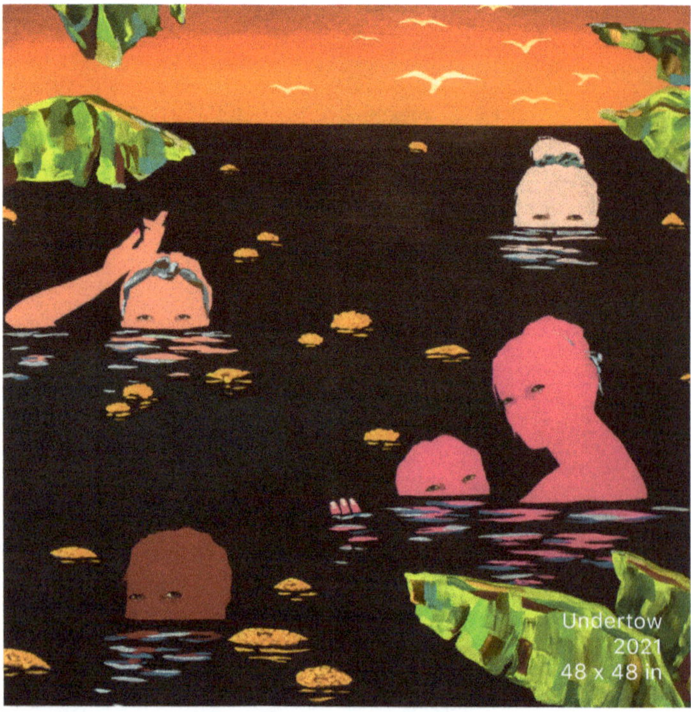

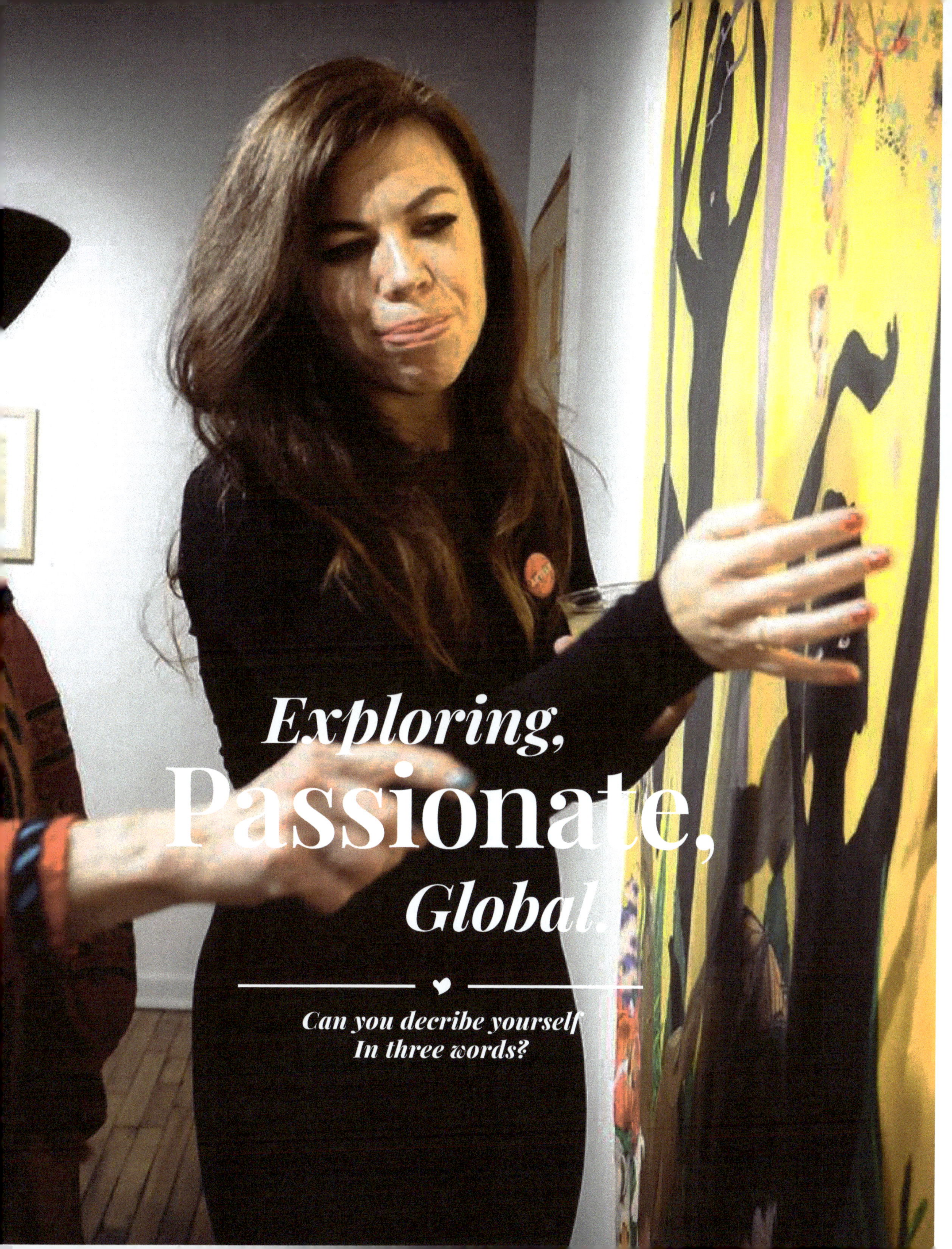

Exploring,
Passionate,
Global.

Can you decribe yourself
In three words?

"You have more power than you think you do."

Caitlin Cartwright is a Detroit-based social change artist whose vibrant narrative works combine painting, drawing, and collage to explore the stories that connect people across cultures and circumstance. Many years spent living and working in locales such as Madagascar, Namibia, India, as well as multiple places within the US, influence both the emotional and geographical scope of her pieces. Caitlin earned her BFA from Maryland Institute College of Art, MICA, as well as a masters degree in sustainable international development from SIT, and completed a six-moth residency at the Pocosin Arts School of Fine Craft in Columbia, NC. She uses art as a storytelling tool for economic empowerment, peace building, and healing and wellness. She has been profiled in Think TV's Emmy winning The Art Show and her work has been featured in such publications as New American Painters, Create Magazine, and Friend of the Artist. She is represented by Brandt Roberts Gallery.

SO, TELL US ABOUT THE WORK YOU MAKE & WHY?
I make work because there are stories that I think need to be told. I'm not a writer or a musician or journalist. I'm an artist, a visual person. Its how I think and express myself, so I tell stories through paintings.

I make figurative narrative paintings that are saturated in color. I use imagery from what's around me. It may be pop culture, textile design, botany, hairstyles. These elements add context to my work. I take inspiration from stories that resonate with me. One example is of a little boy that used to live in a neighboring farm when I was in Namibia. He had a lot of difficulties going on with his family and I would always see him outside with a small group of animals that took care of. They were beautiful, half donkey and half zebra, zebdonks. We became friends and it really stuck with me that while he didn't feel like he could find peace within his home, he was able to find a lot of comfort being with the animals that he loved. When I was back in the states, I was going through some difficult times myself and I kept thinking about this little boy and his zebdonks. I was feeling like I needed to find my own place of comfort and I was able to give that to myself through painting my version of this story.

I make work in hopes that the viewer will see something in the image that connects with their own narrative. I'm a big believer in the idea that the more specific you can get the more global the reach.

WHERE DO YOU FIND YOUR PURPOSE AS AN ARTIST?
I find purpose in the world around me. We live in such a big and incredible place. I've been so lucky to be able to experience different communities, and see so much that's different from how I grew up.

I've been extremely honored to learn the stories of many people from all over the world. While everyone is unique, there is so much that connects us. Getting to this point is where I am most inspired.

WHAT WOULD YOU DO WITH YOUR ART, IF YOU HAD NO FEAR?
Great question! I would show my work in unorthodox places. I love a gallery but I'd really like to see my work blown up huge and shown in the places that inspired it. On the side of a building in a business district or in the dessert, becoming interactive within the environment. I think it would be so exciting to make this happen.

IF YOU HAVE THE WORLD'S ATTENTION FOR 30 SECONDS, WHAT IS THAT YOU WOULD LIKE TO SAY?
I would say that you have more power than you think you do. Identify what your values are and who you want to be. Let that be your guide in every move you make. If you can identify these things, your power is unstoppable.

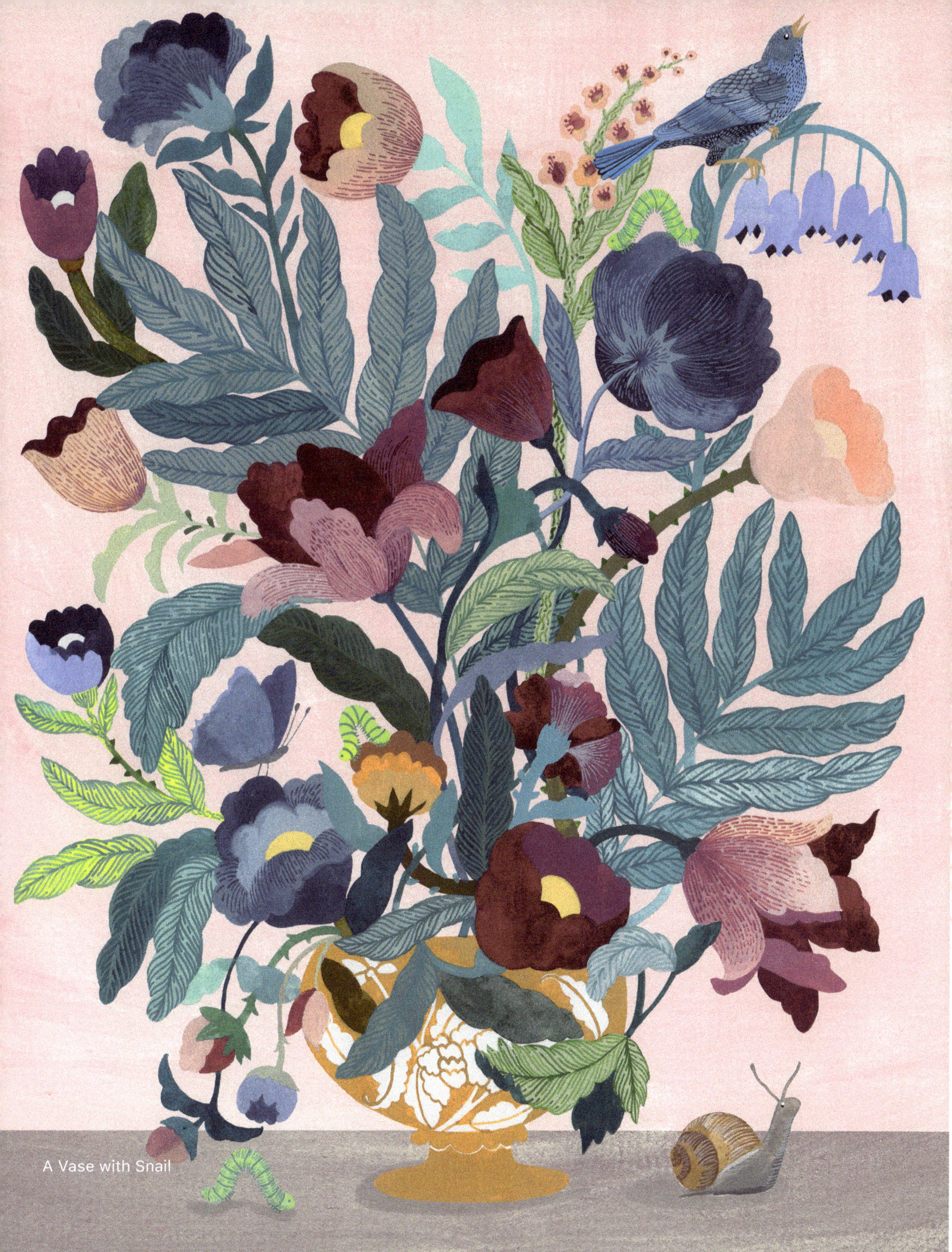

A Vase with Snail

Malin Gyllensvaan

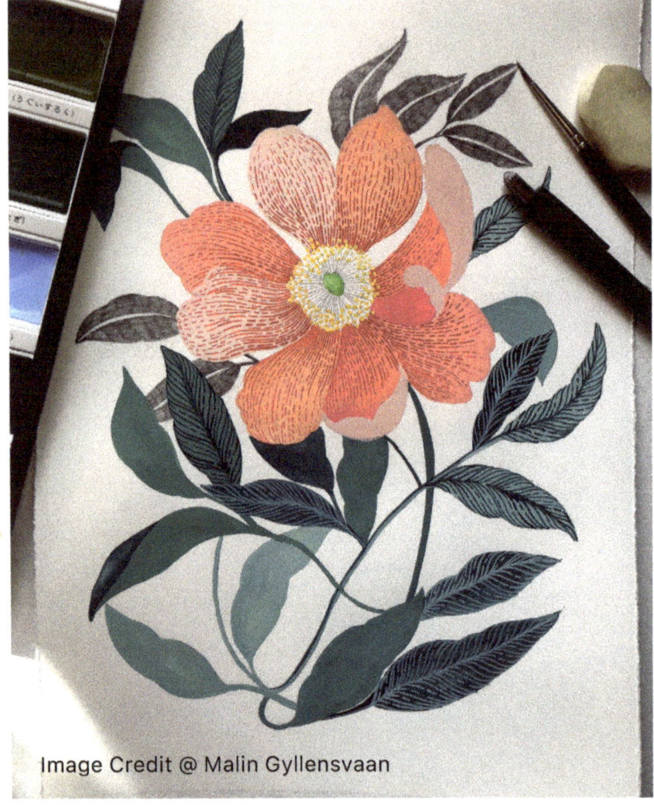

Image Credit @ Malin Gyllensvaan

www.malingyllensvaan.com
@mallengyllensvaan

Malin Gyllensvaan is based in Stockholm,Sweden and has been developed her *lush, ethereal style* since she was a child.

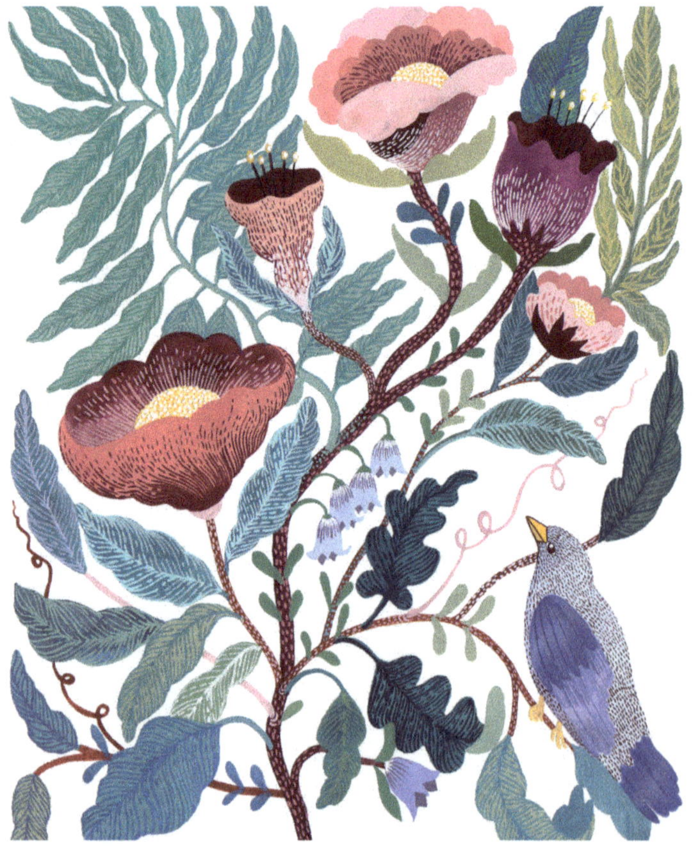

Image Credit @ Malin Gyllensvaan

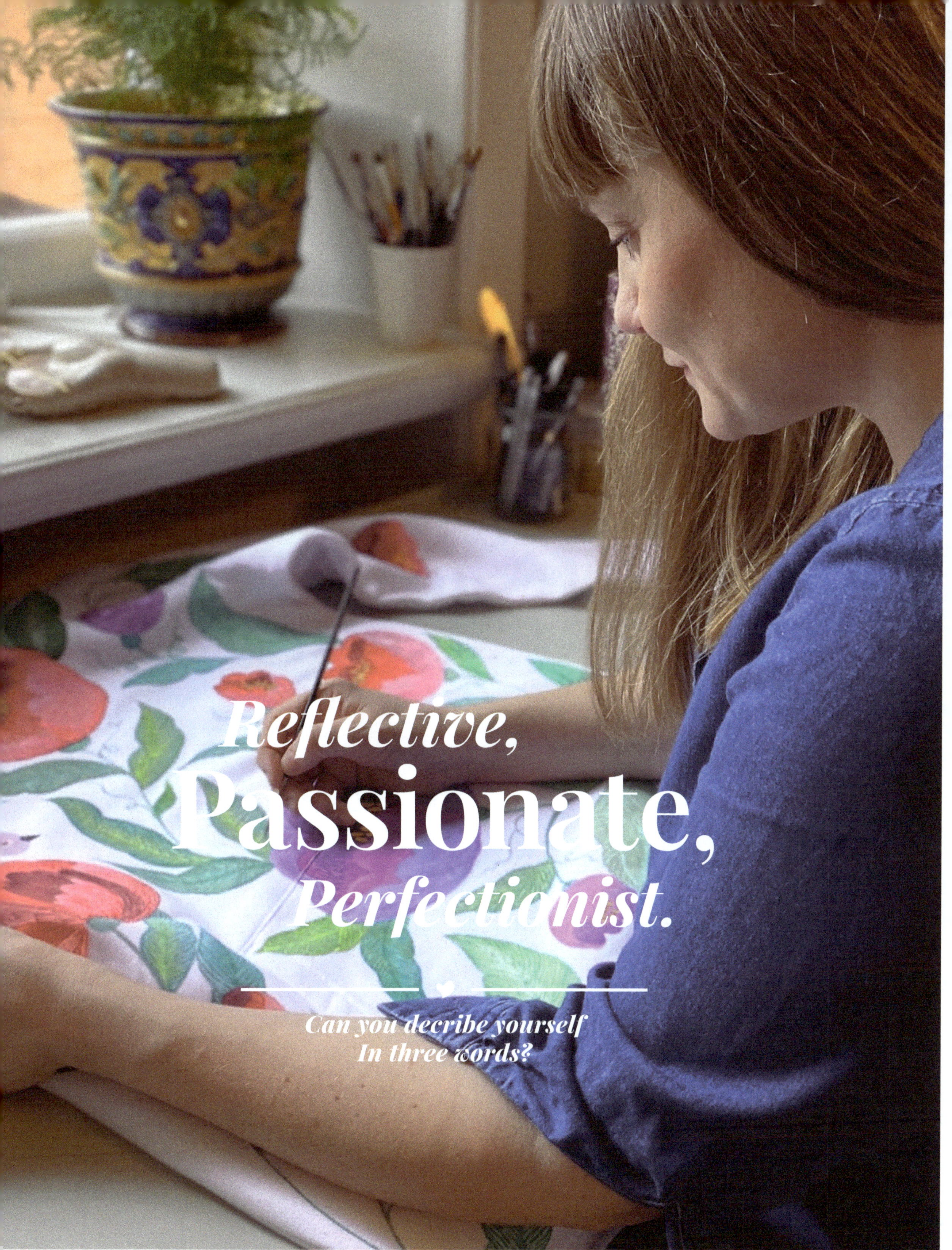

Reflective,
Passionate,
Perfectionist.

Can you decribe yourself
In three words?

WHAT WOULD YOU DO WITH YOUR ART, IF YOU HAD NO FEAR?

I would love to paint really big and slow with lots of details but currently I don't have enough space.
This would also require me saying no to more commissions etc. and potentially loose income and that is always scary!

IF YOU HAVE THE WORLD'S ATTENTION FOR 30 SECONDS, WHAT IS THAT YOU WOULD LIKE TO SAY?

How do we fix this mess??

"How do we fix this mess?"

Malin Gyllensvaan is based in Stockholm,Sweden and has been developed her lush, ethereal style since she was a child.

Inspired by nature, vintage botanical studies and folk art, her illustrations are a homage to the natural world, rendered in pencil and gouache.

Over the years, her creations have adorned everything from paper goods, puzzles, packaging, interior and fashion textiles, as well as illustrations for books.
Her clients include: IKEA, Eeboo, Anthropologie, Bespoke press, Design House Greetings, Holt Renfrew, H&M, Åhléns, Cappelen Damm and Berghs förlag to name a few.

SO, TELL US ABOUT THE WORK YOU MAKE & WHY?

I have a Bachelor in textile design but I see myself as a decorative illustrator or an illustrative textile designer. I love to paint decorative elements but I also have a thought behind my paintings, it might be subtle to some but it's important to me that you can stop for a second and discover hidden things in my paintings.
I paint because I love it and it soothes my soul but my hope is that it will do the same for others who see it.
That their heart will make a little jump and that they will feel inspired to create themselves or just feel some joy however quick.

WHERE DO YOU FIND YOUR PURPOSE AS AN ARTIST?

I have always had a strong sense of needing to use my hands for different kinds of crafts and materials. I express myself like that and it makes me feel like a have a place in the world.
My purpose is found in doing, by constantly creating and trying not to think too much about it. I am much more interested in the process than the original or product. My mind has left it as it's finished and I am on to the next blank paper.

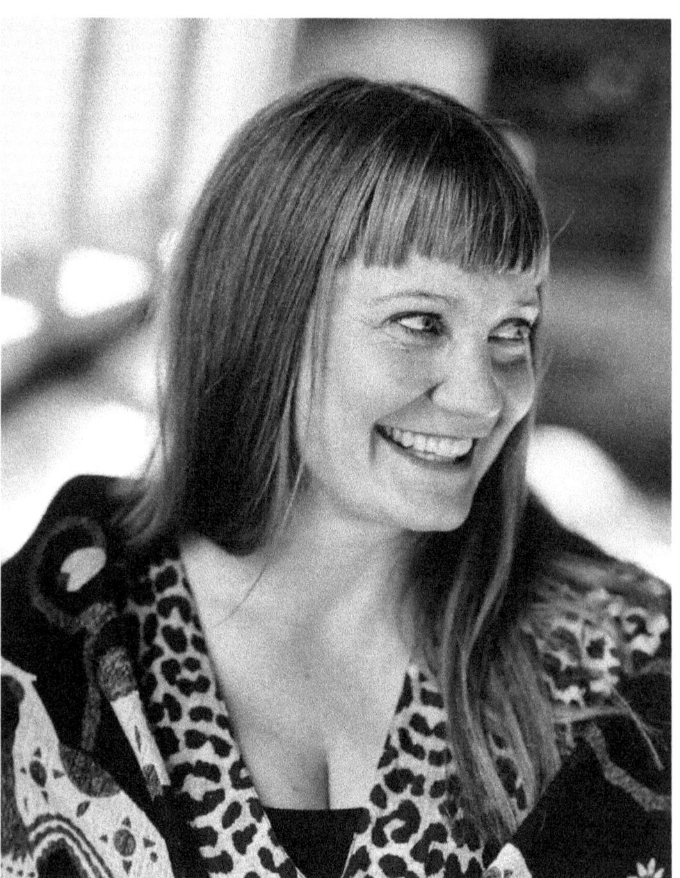

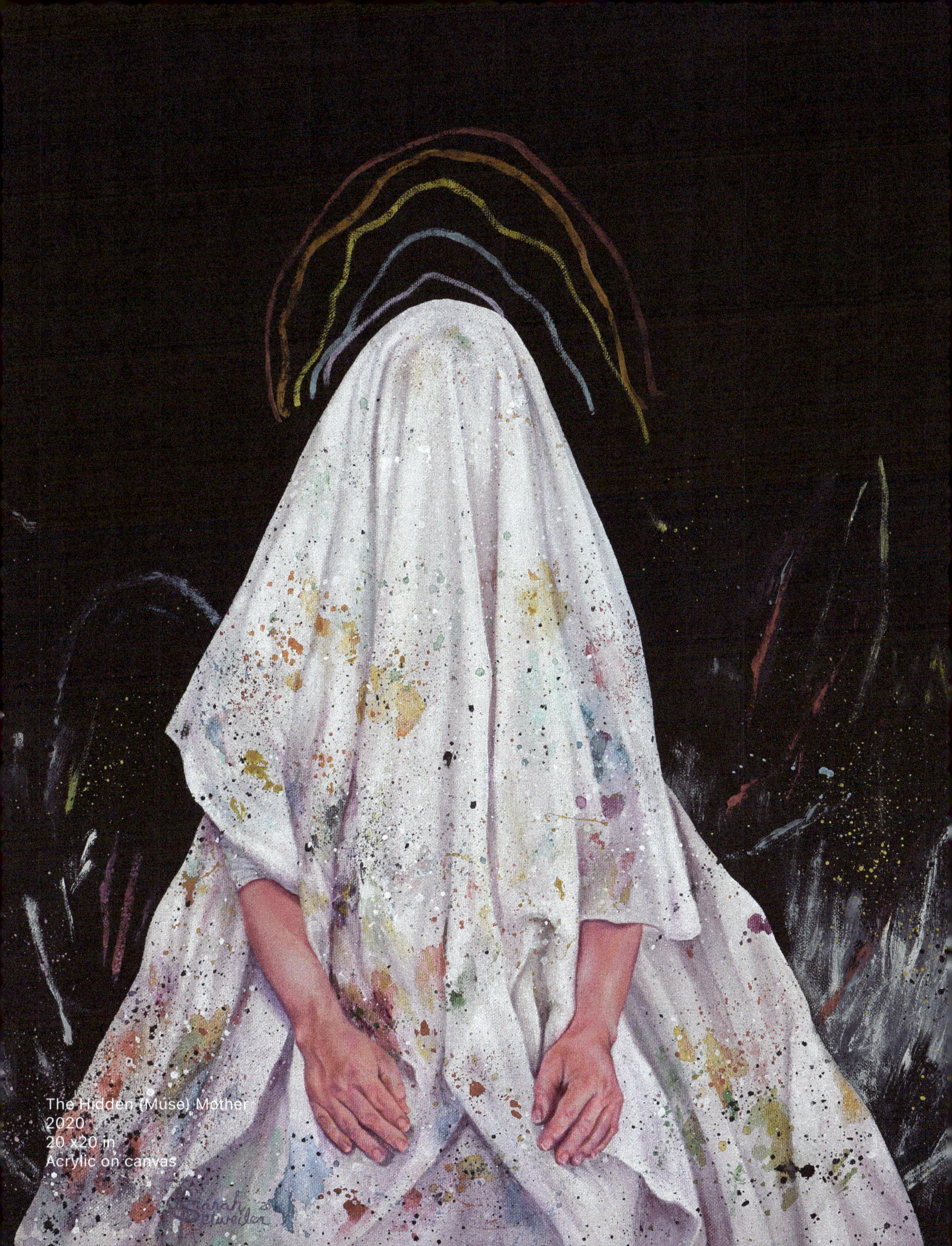
The Hidden (Muse) Mother
2020
20 x20 in
Acrylic on canvas

Sarah Detweiler

Sarah Is a *mixed media artist* from, US who has lived happily in *combining painting* with various *fiber art techniques*, including *hand embroidery, punch needle.*

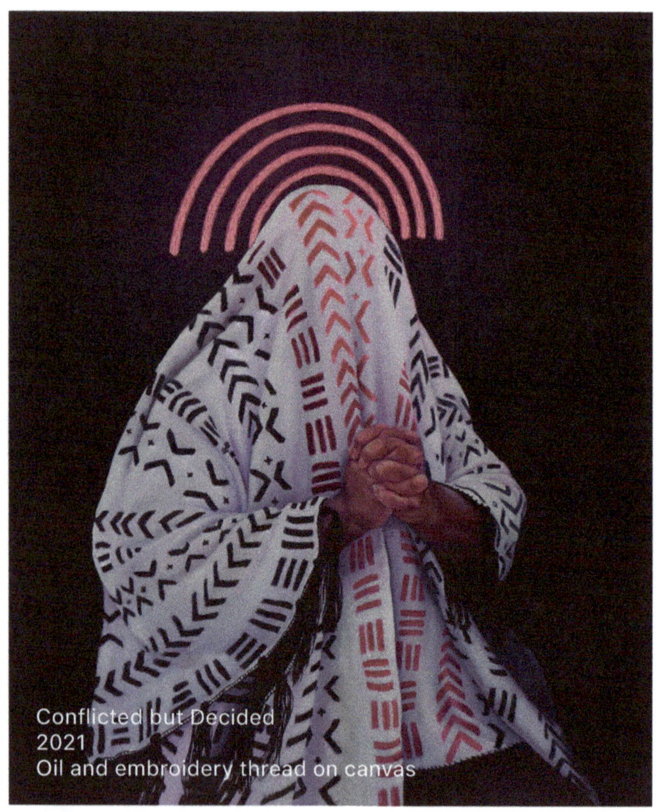

www.sarahdetweiler.com

@sd_artifacts

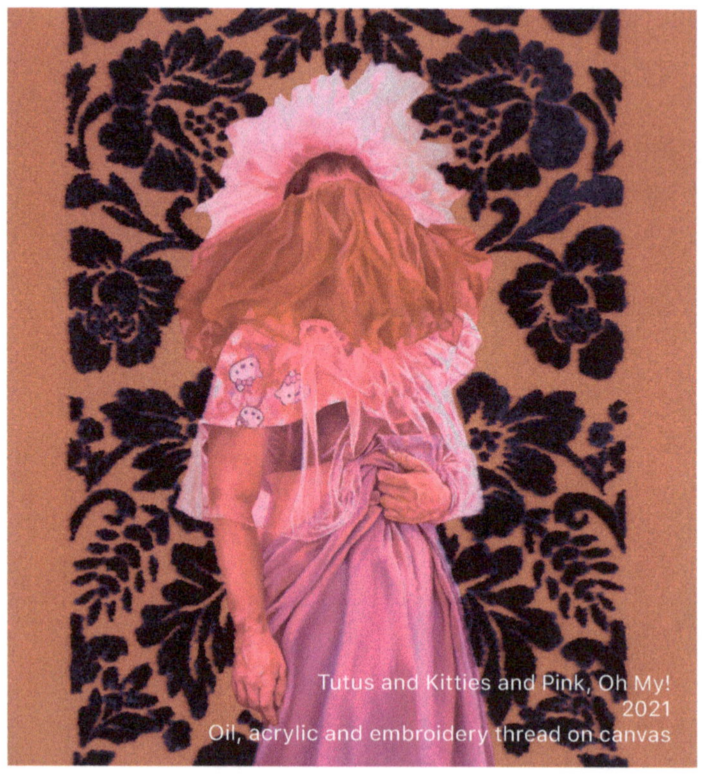

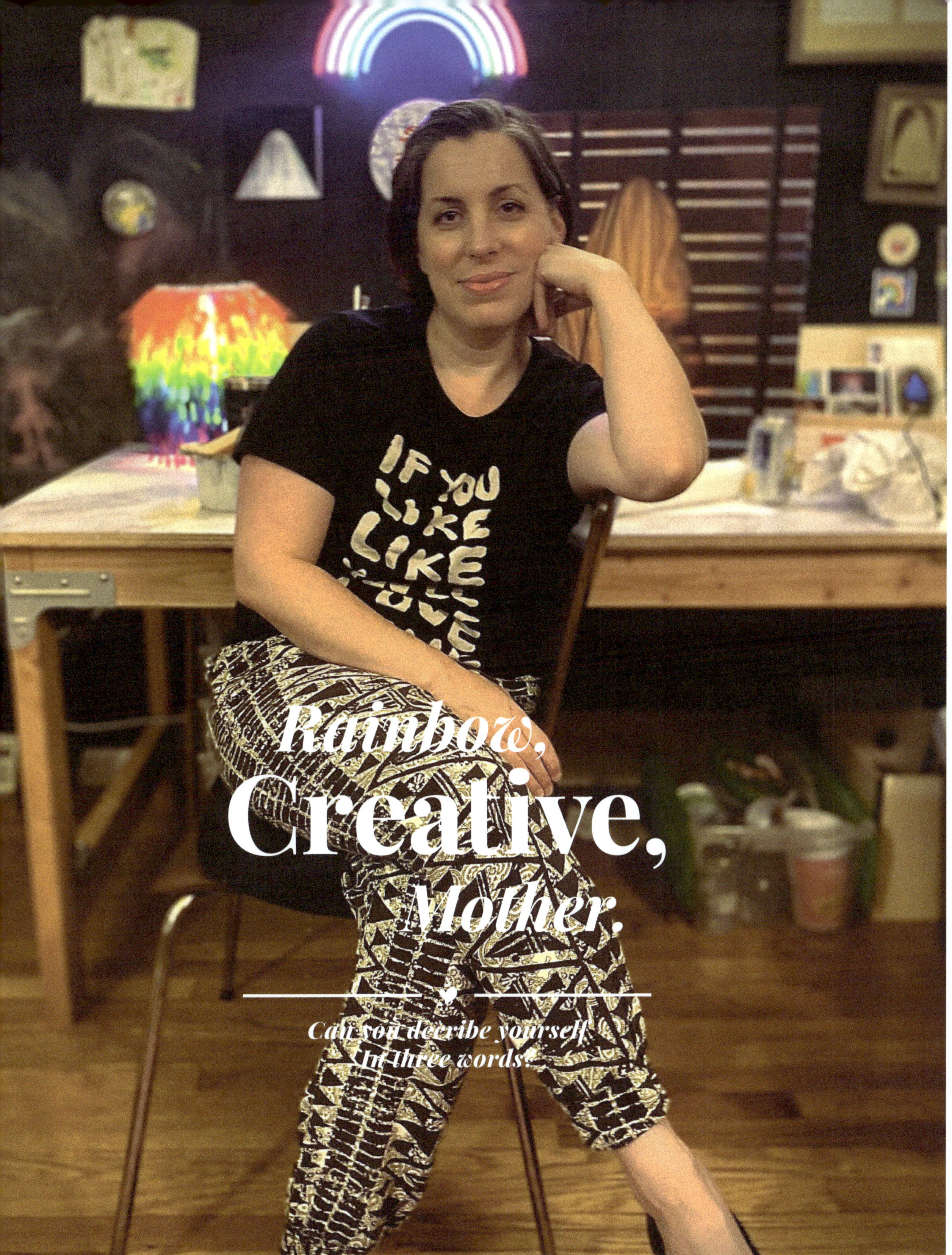
Rainbow,
Creative,
Mother.
Can you decribe yourself
In three words?

"How can I help?"

Sarah Detweiler is a Philadelphia area-based visual artist translating her experiences as a mother into figurative and narrative paintings with hand embroidery. She has a BFA in Visual Communications from University of Delaware and a masters degree in Art Therapy from Pratt. Sarah has shown her work in solo and group exhibits in galleries across the country and virtually. Most notably, her "Hidden Mother" series sold out in two exhibitions with Paradigm Gallery in Philadelphia. Sarah's work has been published in Hi-Fructose, Create, Artit, MILKED, and Uppercase Magazines, and featured on art blogs including Colossal and The Jealous Curator. She has also been interviewed for multiple art podcasts including The Jealous Curator's podcast, Art For Your Ear. Sarah's art centers around themes of nostalgia, motherhood, fertility, and the rainbow as an archetype.

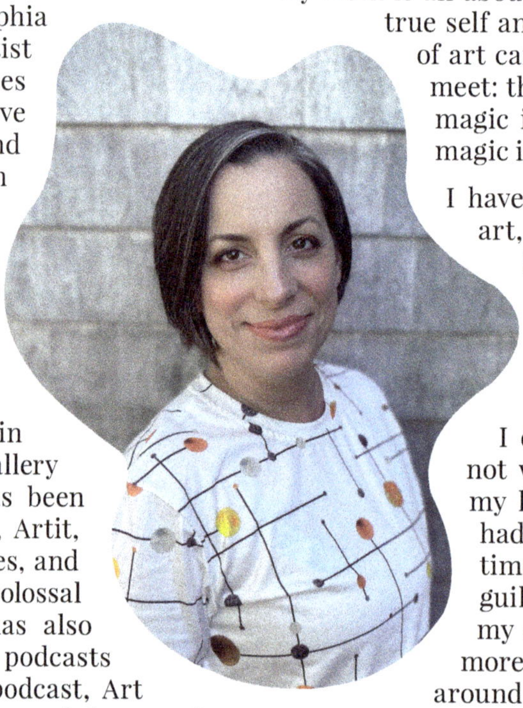

SO, TELL US ABOUT THE WORK YOU MAKE & WHY?

Wherever my artistic practice takes me, it is always rooted in painting. For the past 5 years, my art has lived happily in combining painting with various fiber art techniques, including hand embroidery, punch needle, etc. Including such techniques in my work was the natural course through which I could experiment with the levels and texture of the painting's surface. I love the opportunity to jump back and forth from painting to embroidery. It is where I found my true self.

The subject matter in my art is almost always figurative, but I like to push the boundaries of what is considered a portraiture by often concealing the subject matter with fabric. My work explores narratives between the seen and unseen. The authenticity in my work is typically derived from my own experiences as a mother.

WHERE DO YOU FIND YOUR PURPOSE AS AN ARTIST?

My work is all about connection. Connecting with my true self and connecting with others. A piece of art can become a place where two souls meet: the creator and the viewer. There is magic in that moment. But there is also magic in the moments that lead up to it.

I have always found many purposes in art, but the most important is its healing nature. I am in my happy place when I inspire others to create.

WHAT WOULD YOU DO WITH YOUR ART, IF YOU HAD NO FEAR?

I don't think fear is my issue. It is not what limits me. In this season of my life, time is my nemesis. If I only had more time. I would spend more time in my studio without feeling guilty that it is taking time away from my children. I would say yes to many more opportunities. I would travel around the world to visit artist friends and work on collaborations with them. I would do residencies and attend more openings. I would experiment with process without being under the pressure of a deadline. But most importantly, I would make more work.

IF YOU HAVE THE WORLD'S ATTENTION FOR 30 SECONDS, WHAT IS THAT YOU WOULD LIKE TO SAY?

How can I help? And then I would spend the next 27 seconds listening.

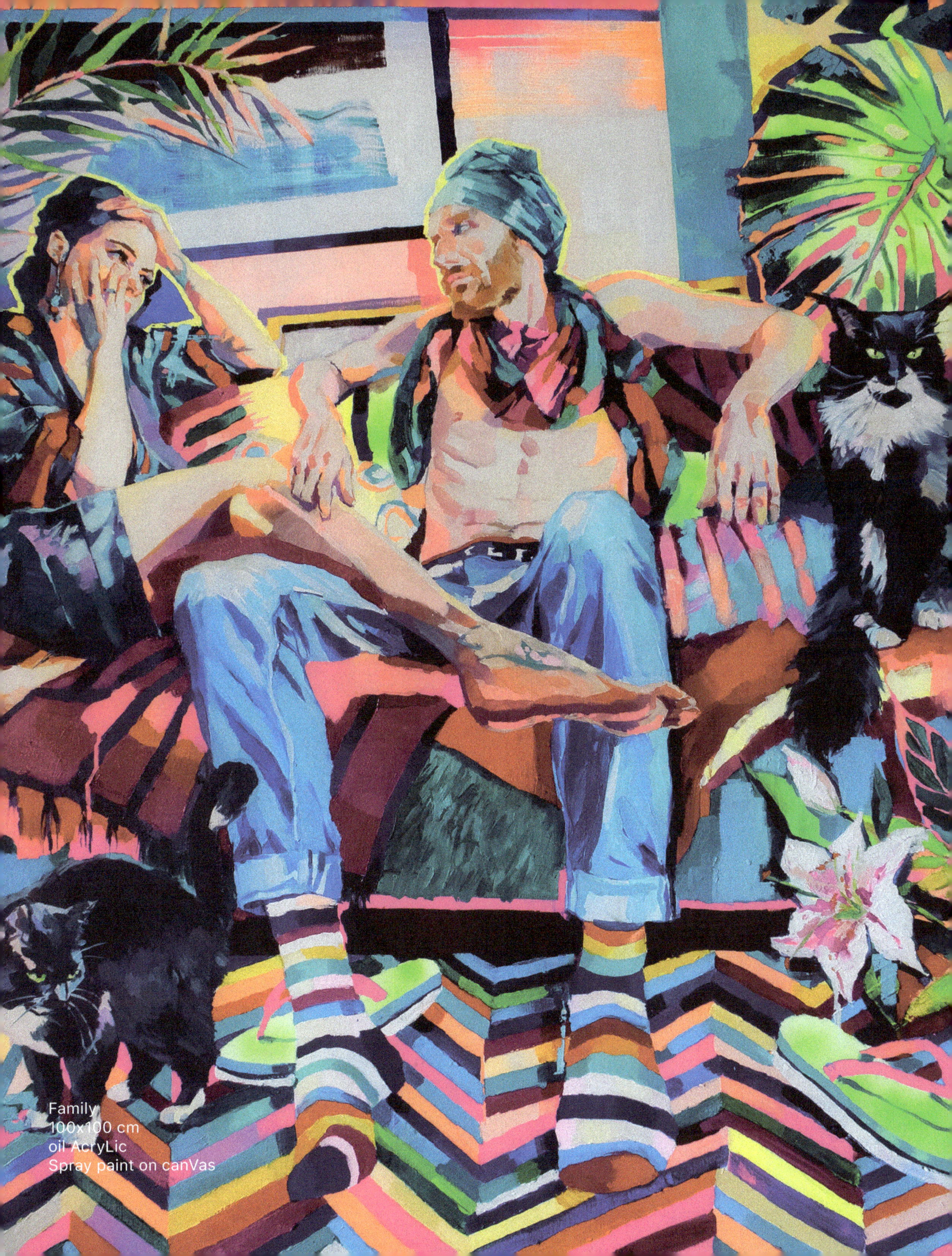

Family
100x100 cm
oil AcryLic
Spray paint on canVas

Joanna Pilarczyk

A London-based *contemporary figurative painter* and *art educator*. She paints *relaxing atmosphere, intimacy, femininity, self-awareness* and her *relationship* with nature.

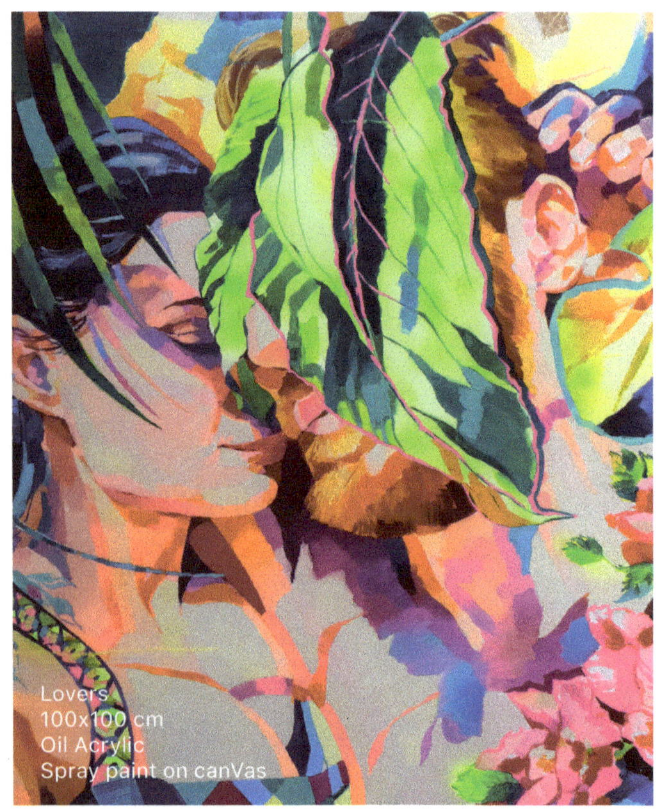

www.joannapilarczyk.com

@joannapilarczyk

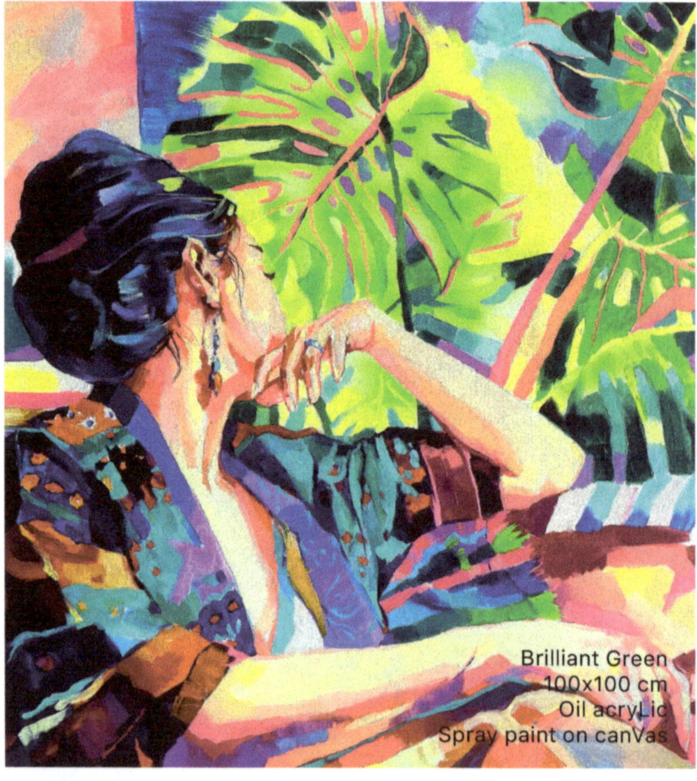

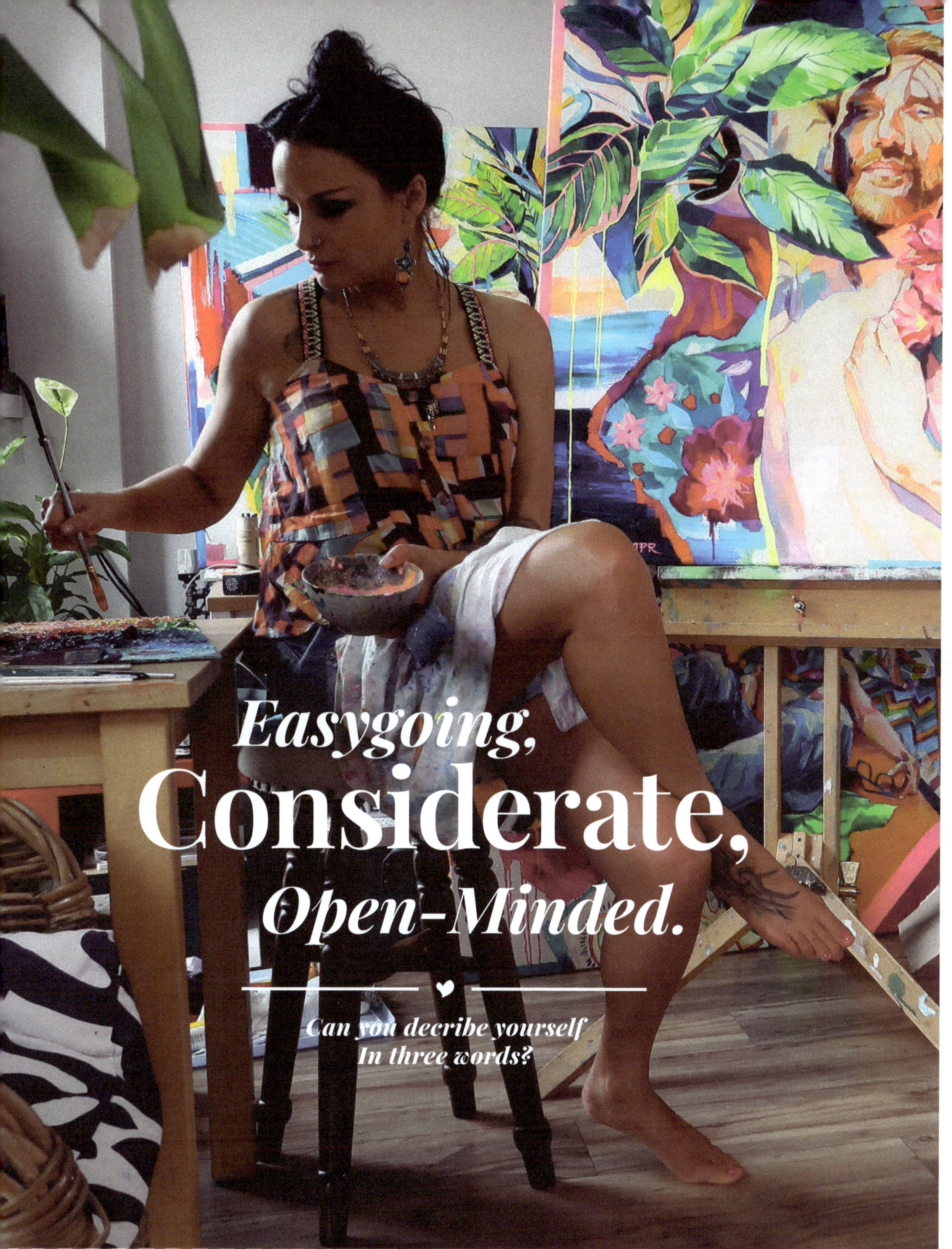

Easygoing,
Considerate,
Open-Minded.

Can you decribe yourself
In three words?

"Slow down, look around, take a breath, admire beauty of nature."

Joanna studied at the Art University in Zielona Gora. She holds MA degree in Visual Arts and Art Education. After moving to London over a decade ago, Joanna fell in love with the city immediately. Amazed and entranced by diverse cultures and the vibrant energy, Joanna began to paint oil portraits of new acquaintances and friends within the artist community of North London.

In her recent vibrant paintings, she focusses on a relaxing atmosphere, intimacy, femininity, self-awareness and her relationship with nature. She says 'I want the viewer to notice a simple reasons to be happy, feel the warm sunlight on their skin, smell the sweet fragrance of the flowers and admire beauty and vibrant colours of surrounding life.

Pilarczyk is a finalist of Women United Art Prize 2021. She has exhibited her work nationally and internationally. Her paintings have been featured in various global art exhibitions and contemporary art publications including: Create! Magazine, All She Makes, Art Seen, The Huts and New Visionary Magazine.

SO, TELL US ABOUT THE WORK YOU MAKE & WHY?

My vivid paintings celebrate and explore the subject of femininity, intimacy, love and my relationship with nature. As a figurative painter I take my inspiration from people often focusing on female figure resting in a vibrant, colourful dream-like garden, somewhere between imagined and reality.

Colour is the main reason why I am drawn to art. It's my emotional response and toll to showcase a specific atmosphere in my paintings.

Born in Poland in 1980, times of the greatest economic crisis in my country, I remember days when everything seemed to be grey and life of my family difficult for many years.

Creativity was a form of my personal escape from monotony of my surroundings. First breaks of Western culture appearing in TV had started my fascination by Hollywood movies and vibrancy of 'idillic' American world.

Characteristic neon colours, beautiful flowers and plants, sunlight reflecting on the resting bodies and the atmosphere os serenity began to dominate my canvas since breakdown of Pandemic

In the recent series 'My Paradise' I explore subject of leisure, self-awareness, ease, and meditation. In my new paintings I also convey a stillness. A moment where the subjects are simply being, and free of responsibility.

However this sits in contrast to the vibrant energetic colours. I want the view to be drawn in by the often dynamic compositions, the lure of the colours, and then notice the stillness set within that.

My paintings serve me as a protective barrier from gloom and escalating cruelty in the world.

WHERE DO YOU FIND YOUR PURPOSE AS AN ARTIST?

I find inspiration among people. I have been always fascinated by human anatomy, beauty of our bodies and faces. During my student days in Poland and later when I moved to multicultural London, people have been my biggest source of inspiration. I love to paint portraits but also to make an observation of every day life and my close envirament.

A couple of years ago, particularly through the period of lockdown, my work became very personal, of me and my husband at home. As the world has opened up again, my work has become less about us and more about the human experience. In recent paintings we see hands and limbs, which still communicate the idea of leisure and rest through their poses, but we see less of the sitters faces. This is a way of making the paintings less of a personal story and more universal, where the viewer is invited to fill in the gaps as they view the work, and perhaps even see themselves in the setting.

WHAT WOULD YOU DO WITH YOUR ART, IF YOU HAD NO FEAR?

I would love to paint much bigger paintings and have an opportunity to show them in various galleries also outside of UK.

I would travel to United States, Australia or Asia and exhibit my art in more suitable places where my paintings could complemet their vibrant, exotic environment.

IF YOU HAVE THE WORLD'S ATTENTION FOR 30 SECONDS, WHAT IS THAT YOU WOULD LIKE TO SAY?

Slow down, look around, take a breath, admire beauty of nature, care for it and respect it.

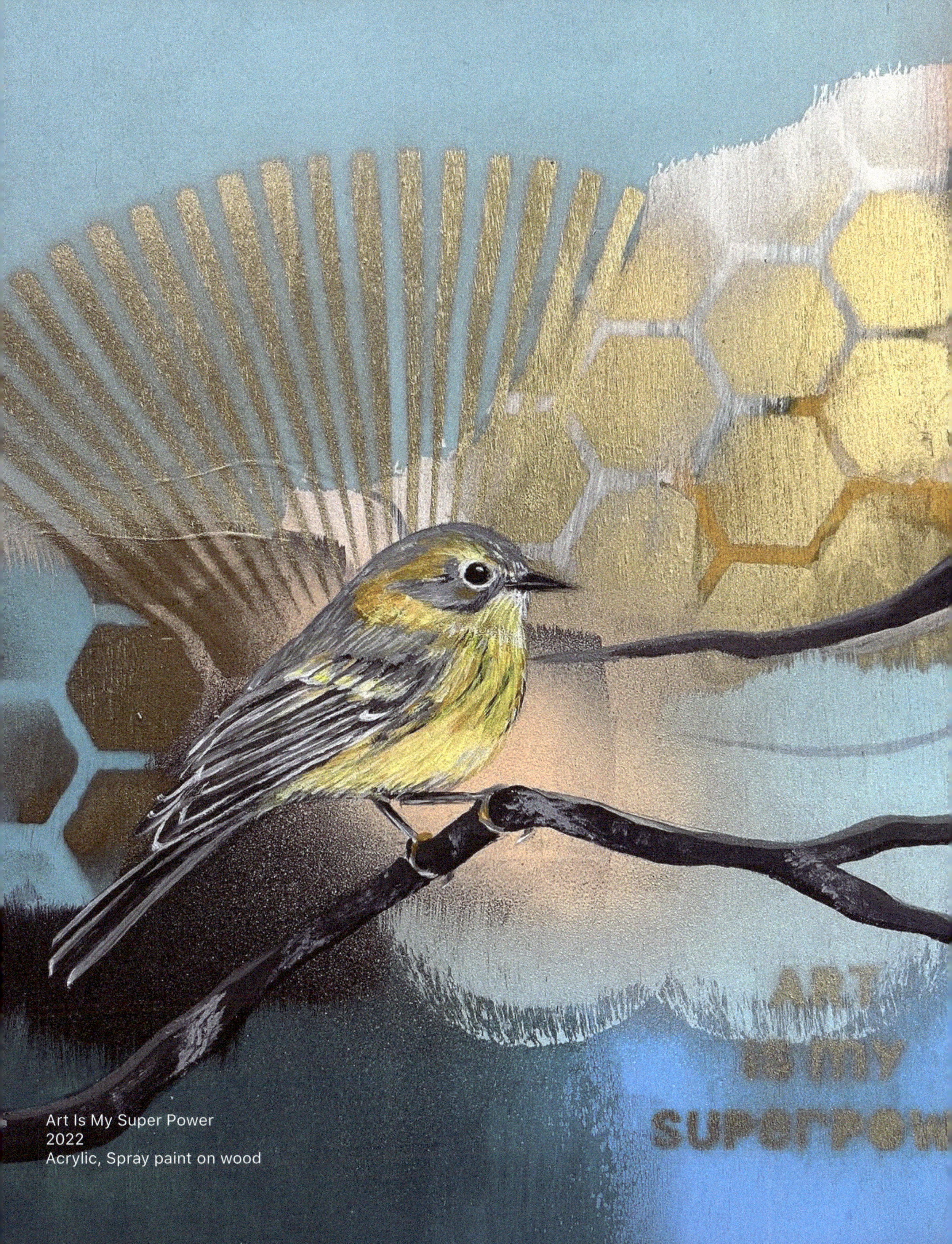

Art Is My Super Power
2022
Acrylic, Spray paint on wood

Leah Guzman

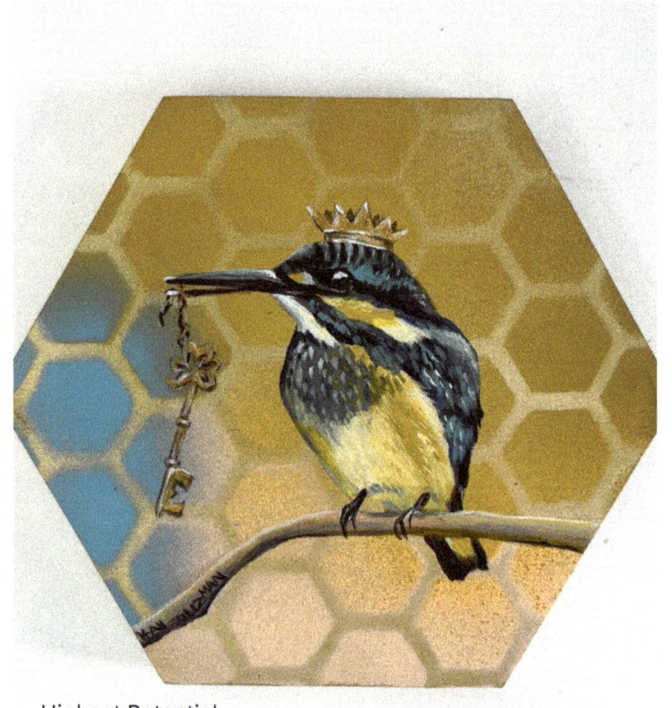

Highest Potential
2022
Acrylic, Spray paint on wood

www.leahguzman.com
@leah.guzman.art

Leah Guzman is a *professional artist* and *Board Certified Art Therapist.* Leah is a *mixed media painter* whose style is *contemporary, symbolic,* and *spirited in nature.*

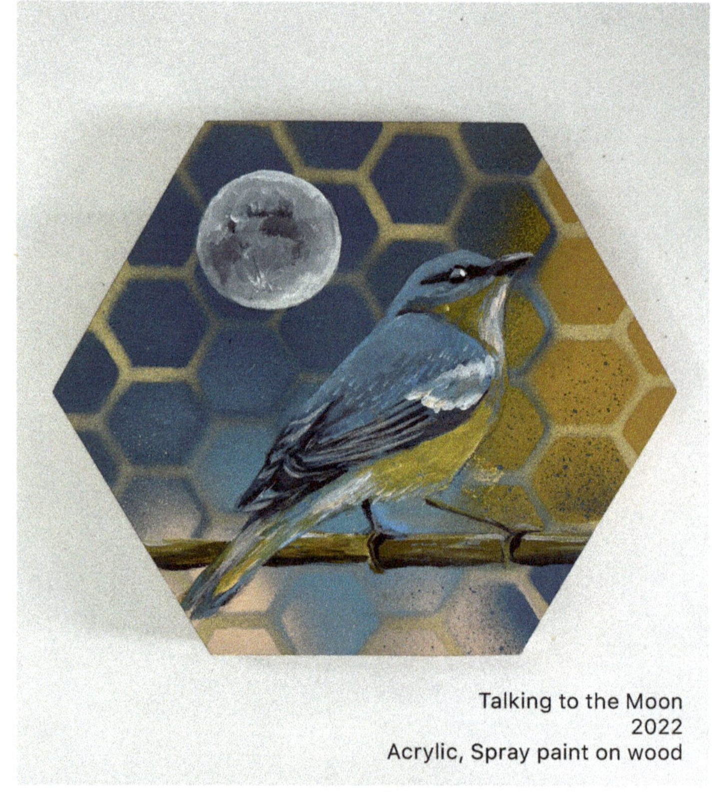

Talking to the Moon
2022
Acrylic, Spray paint on wood

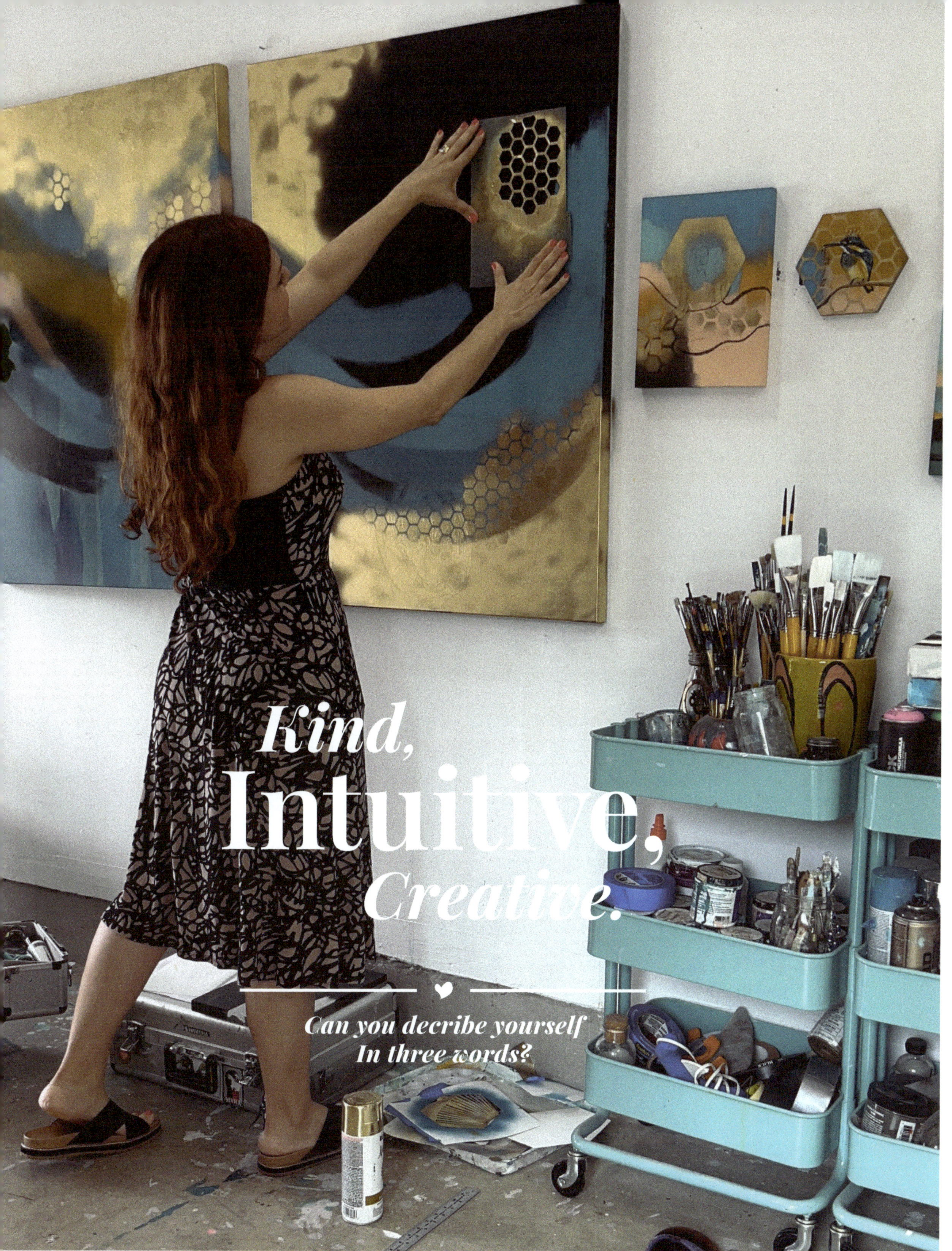

Kind,
Intuitive,
Creative.

Can you decribe yourself
In three words?

Leah Guzman is a professional artist and Board Certified Art Therapist. Leah is a mixed media painter whose style is contemporary, symbolic, and spirited in nature. As an art therapist her mission is to support creatives as a way to heal and manifest their most authentic self and best life. She provides online art therapy sessions and programs. She teaches tools to create a self-care practice and use art a way to for self-development.

SO, TELL US ABOUT THE WORK YOU MAKE & WHY?

The Higher Self Series is an exploration of my spiritual journey with flora, fauna and sacred geometry. My inspiration comes from my lush backyard and my spiritual practice. I see the birds as messengers from Source giving us signs on our journey to show up as our highest selves.

WHERE DO YOU FIND YOUR PURPOSE AS AN ARTIST?

My purpose comes from knowing I feel good when I create art. There have been times where I haven't honored my creative practice and emotionally I didn't feel as good. Creating is an act of self-love. It's an opportunity to tune in and have fun.

WHAT WOULD YOU DO WITH YOUR ART, IF YOU HAD NO FEAR?

I'd love to get back into making sculptures. I have a bachelor of fine arts in sculpture. Some where along the way, a couple poor critiques I stopped expressing myself through 3-d media. I'd love to conquer this fear and turn my paintings into sculptures.

IF YOU HAVE THE WORLD'S ATTENTION FOR 30 SECONDS, WHAT IS THAT YOU WOULD LIKE TO SAY?

Take time daily to check in with your feelings. As creatives we have the opportunity to use art as a superpower. It's a way for us to heal, release and it's a way to use it to manifest our best lives.

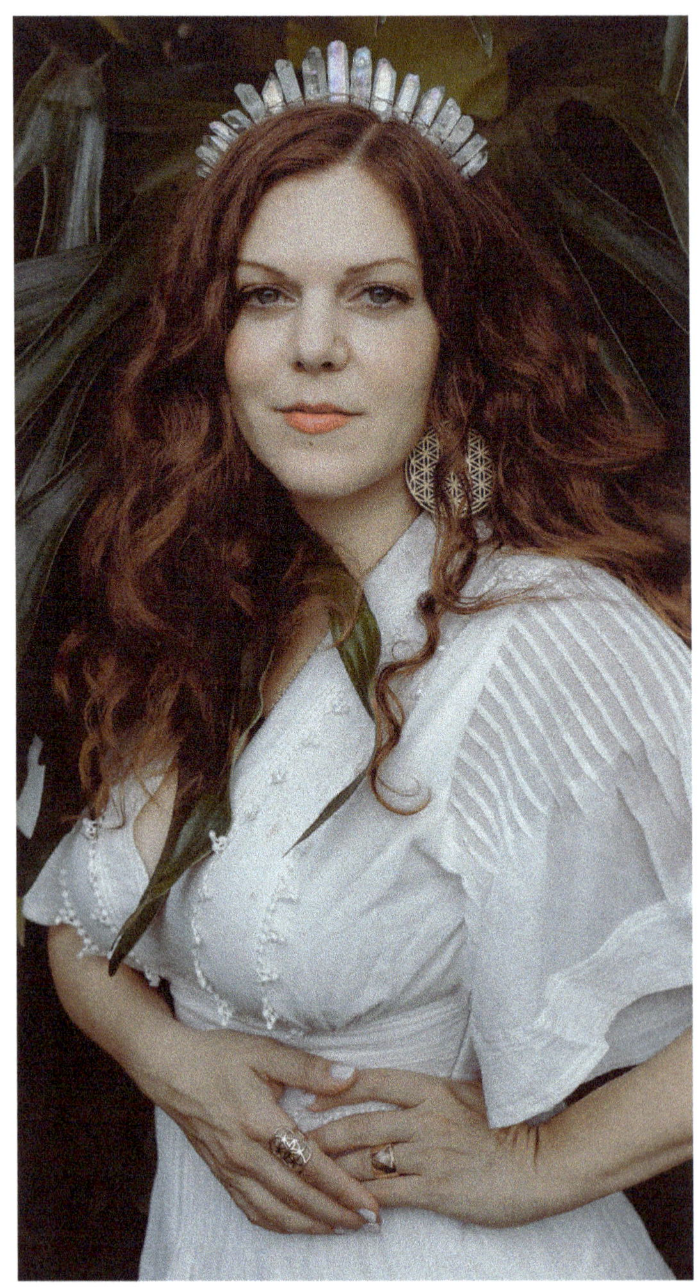

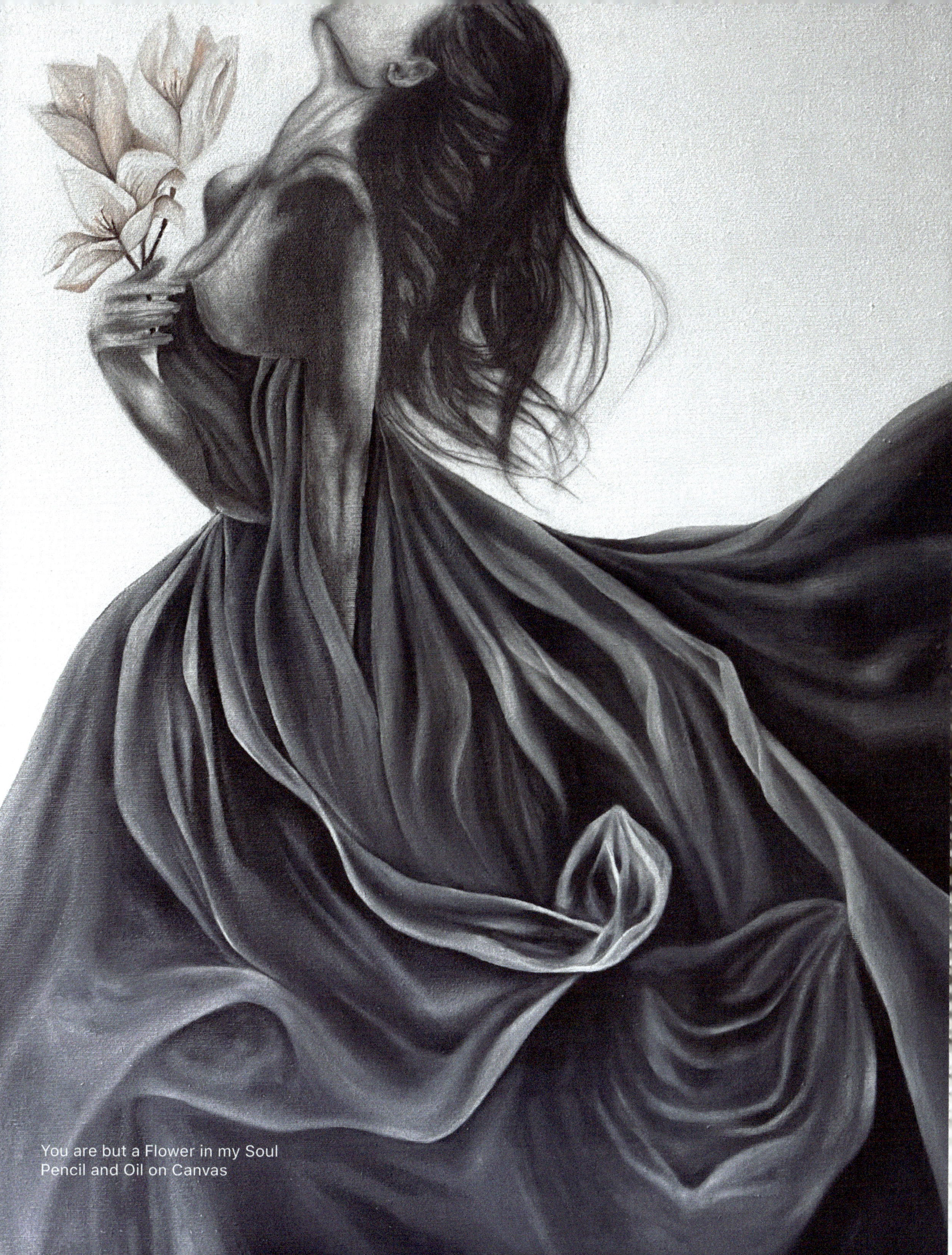

You are but a Flower in my Soul
Pencil and Oil on Canvas

Rachel Le Roux

A British-Filipina *multidisciplinary fine artist* and *interior designer* based in Manila Philippines. She is known mostly for her *love* of the *female form*, most especially of those in motion.

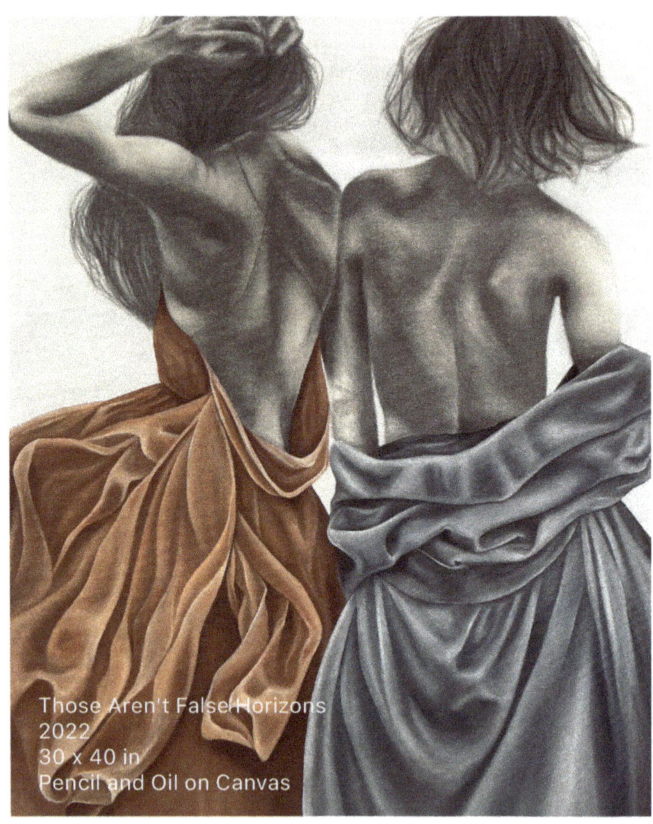

https://www.rlerouxart.com
@rlerouxart

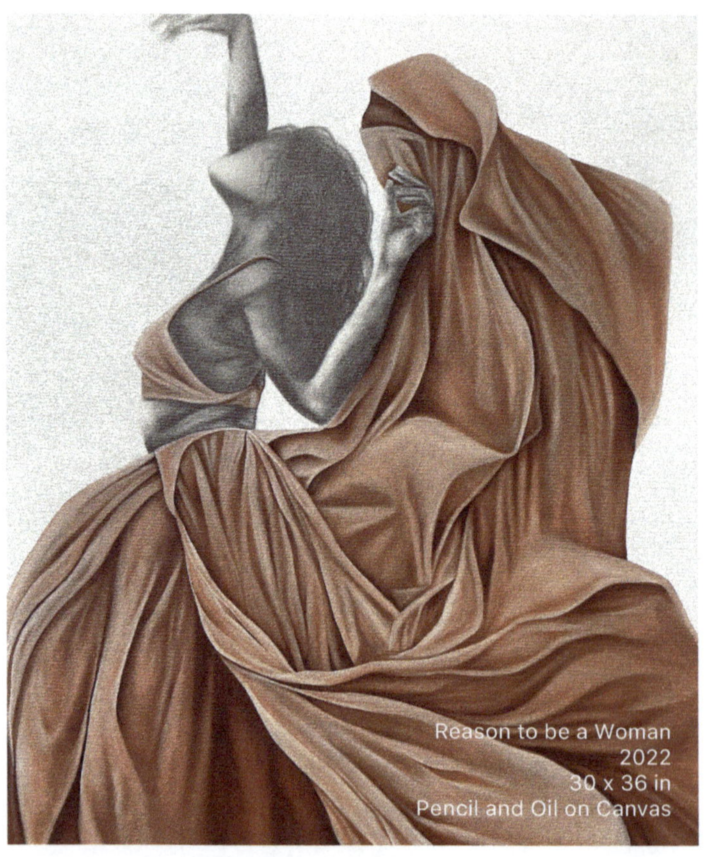

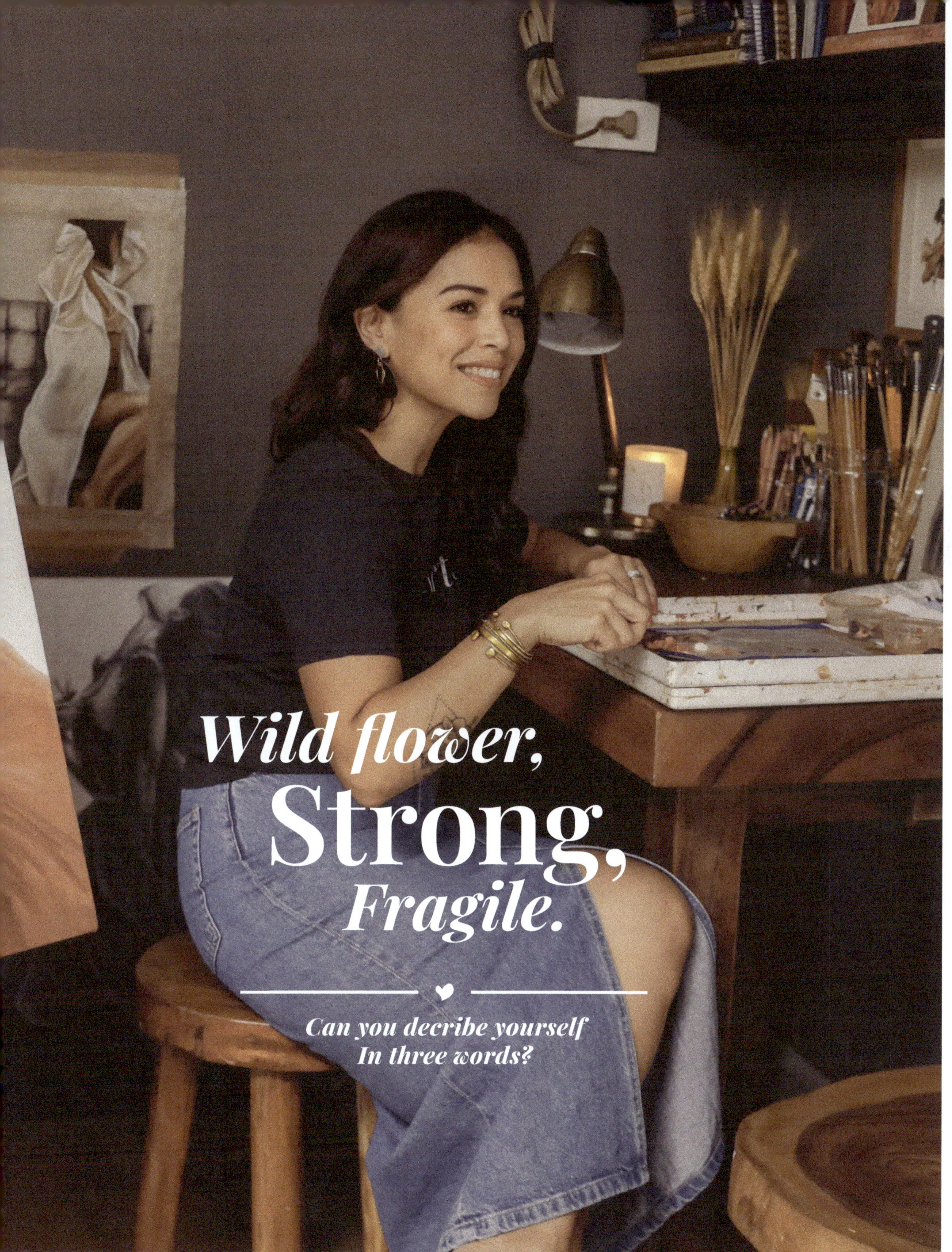

Wild flower,
Strong,
Fragile.

Can you decribe yourself
In three words?

"I would remind the world about love."

A Graduate in BA Honours Degree in Interior and Spatial Design from Chelsea College of Art from London, Working primarily with pencil and oil on canvas, Rachel is known mostly for her love of the female form, most especially of those in motion. In creating each piece, body language and fabric mould together in their own feminine fluidity, holding hidden emotions within the depth of each fold. She has also revisited her abstract art practice and brings her unused paint from her figurative work into play as she continues to explore movement in her abstract pieces. She nurtures her love for both disciplines, creating balance and harmony that is woven into her art practice. The ebb and flow of her growth as an artist remains constant, resonating in the emotional expression exposed in her work.

Rachel's work has been shown in online and local group exhibits, the South Arts Festival Art Fairs, an art auction at Leon Gallery in Manila and her paintings can be found in private collections in the USA, Australia, London, Singapore, Cape Town, Dubai and Manila.

Her work has been featured in Art Seen Magazine and Clover + Bee Magazine.

SO, TELL US ABOUT THE WORK YOU MAKE & WHY?

My art comes from a place that is inspired by the idea of how time is ceaseless, even if your own life feels like it is at a standstill. The figures I draw and dresses I paint express the intensity of an ordinary moment that suddenly becomes an extraordinary one just by pausing in that surrounding chaos. In saying that, with the two disciplines I combine in my practice, they become two contradictory parts of me that make a whole.

In the ladies, I paint them in pencils and oil. My narrative - is hidden in the body movement or in the fabric. Without having to paint faces, one can imagine the single second where that gaze is held momentarily. You know, the one that grasps the absolute essence of a moment? It's like the world keeps on moving but you stop looking around and ultimately just gaze into yourself.

WHERE DO YOU FIND YOUR PURPOSE AS AN ARTIST?

A few months after I turned forty, the pandemic hit. So many unknowns were looming over my head like a dark cloud you couldn't see through. My interior design business couldn't function due to all the hard lockdowns and life just stopped, as if it hit a brick wall dead on. In this time of extremely dark shadows that hovered over me, there were new questions in my life that were brought into the light. One of them was «In everything that is happening, what makes me genuinely happy and authentically whole? It was a realisation that crept up like how blood slowly courses through veins. But when that moment came, it was like the breath that I had been holding onto for so long was finally let go. Art always played a huge part in my creative life for many years, it was there when I needed it. However, it was never something that I chose as the solid core to my being. It was never my backbone, nor was it the biggest slice of the pie of my life. But, deep down, I always knew the reason why I never let it go. It was because art was always my true purpose in my life. And in finding this within myself, eventually it led to finding my whole purpose as an ARTIST.

WHAT WOULD YOU DO WITH YOUR ART, IF YOU HAD NO FEAR?

Perhaps if I had no fear, my art could be tracing the outskirts of each part of the world. If I had no fear, I could have been immersed in a life dictated by art, swallowed whole by a world outside of what has been laid in front of me. If I had no fear, I think I would've been a whole different person who turned their dreams into reality at an earlier stage of my life. If I had no fear, maybe I would've been a muralist painting on the sides of buildings. Maybe I would've been a sculptor. I could be painting intricate details of ethnic fabrics on large canvas. Or possibly, I could've thrown myself out of my whole periphery and I could've even been stage set designer in the middle of Broadway or the West End. {The latter was a silent dream job for years by the way.}

So I think I need this fear for me to explore the process even further and honestly, I am okay with not really knowing what my art would be like if that fear didn't trace every outline of my being.

IF YOU HAVE THE WORLD'S ATTENTION FOR 30 SECONDS, WHAT IS THAT YOU WOULD LIKE TO SAY?

I think I would remind the world about love - love for and from the people who make up your your trie or your core, but also of love for the people who also just simply skim the surface around you. Love in being gentle and kind with yourself and love for your own skills and capabilities too. I would also speak of the love for your faults, your broken parts, your fractures and cracks but I would remind you of your capacity to emerge through that all.

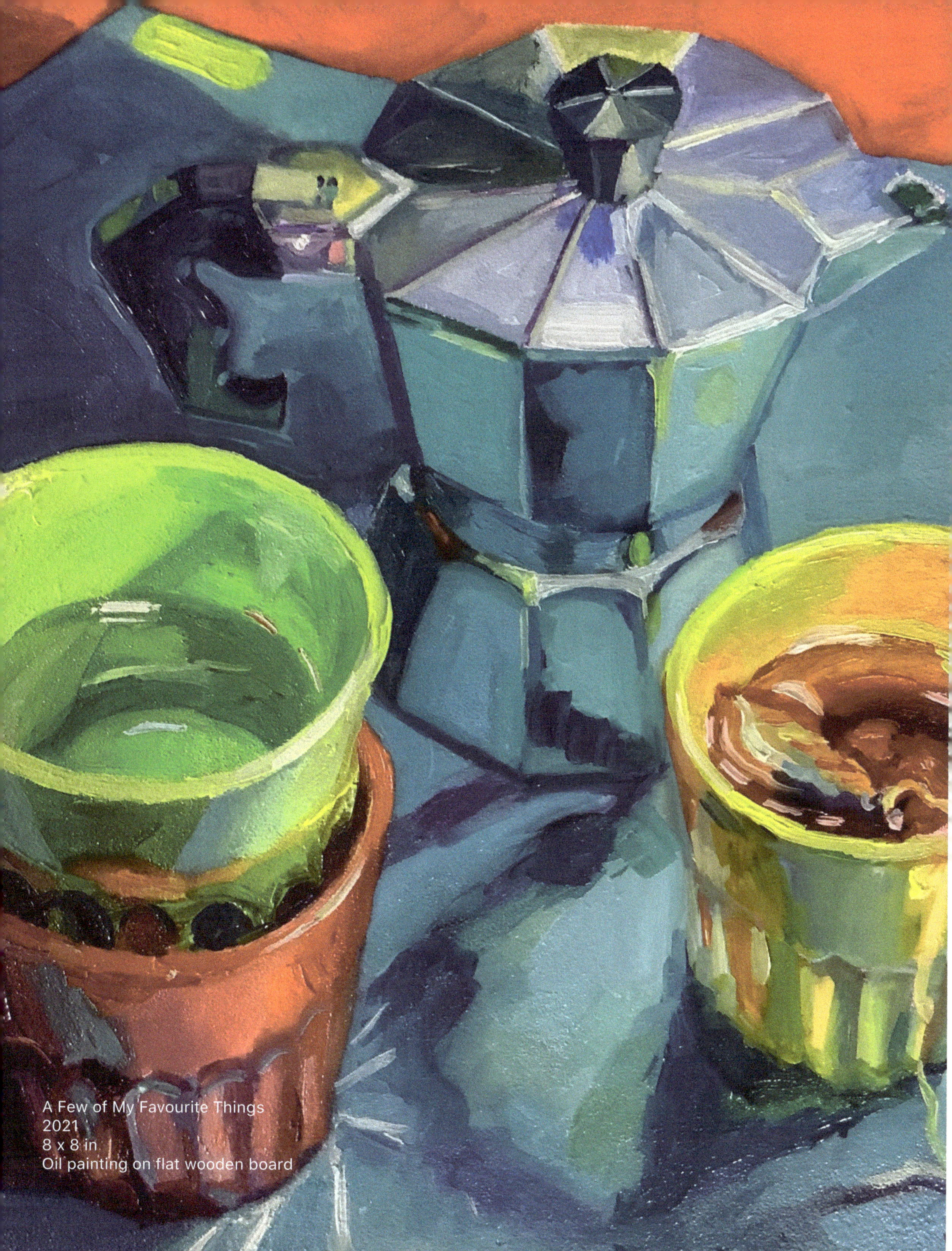
A Few of My Favourite Things
2021
8 x 8 in
Oil painting on flat wooden board

Fatema Ibrahim

Fatema is a Bangalore based *Fine Artist* specialising in *oil painting*. She enjoys *painting food*, things at home and her surroundings and places she has visited.

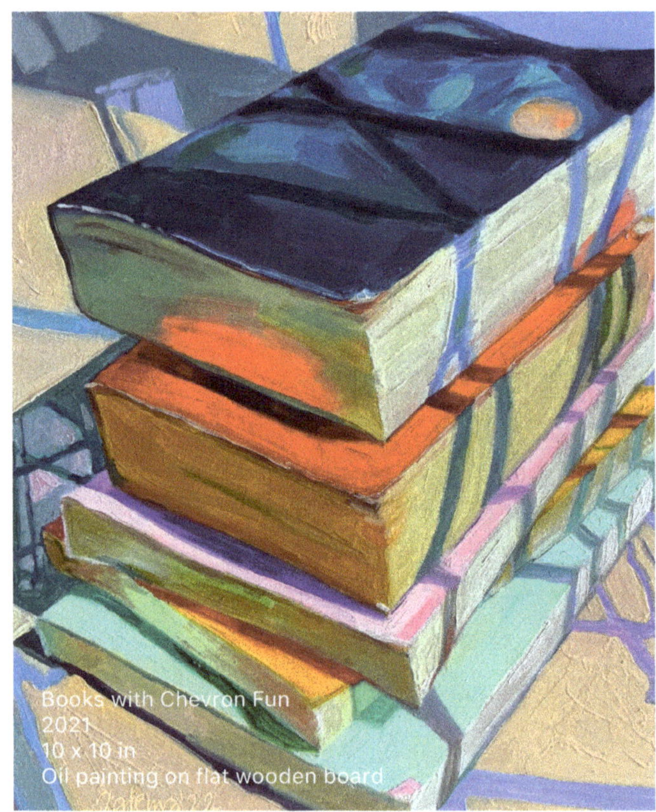

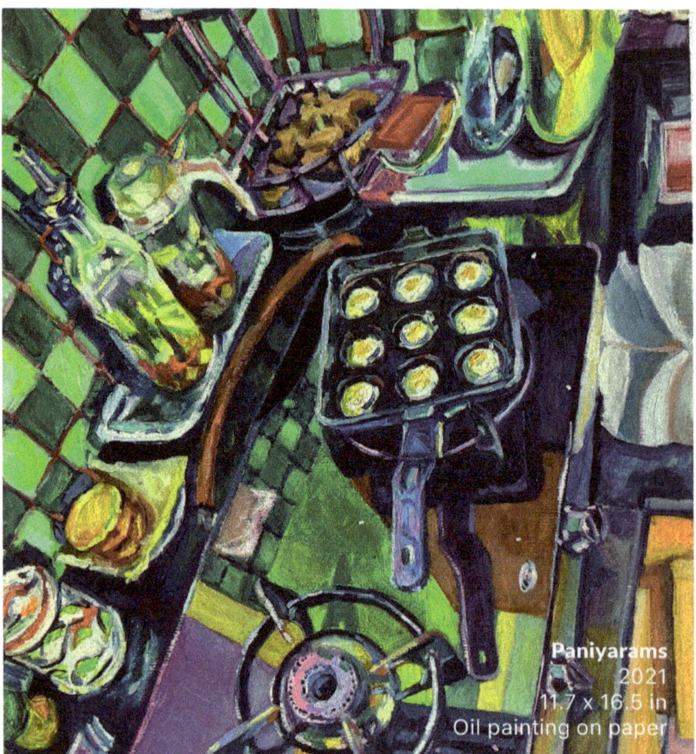

Instagram.com/fatemaibrahimart
@fatemaibrahimart

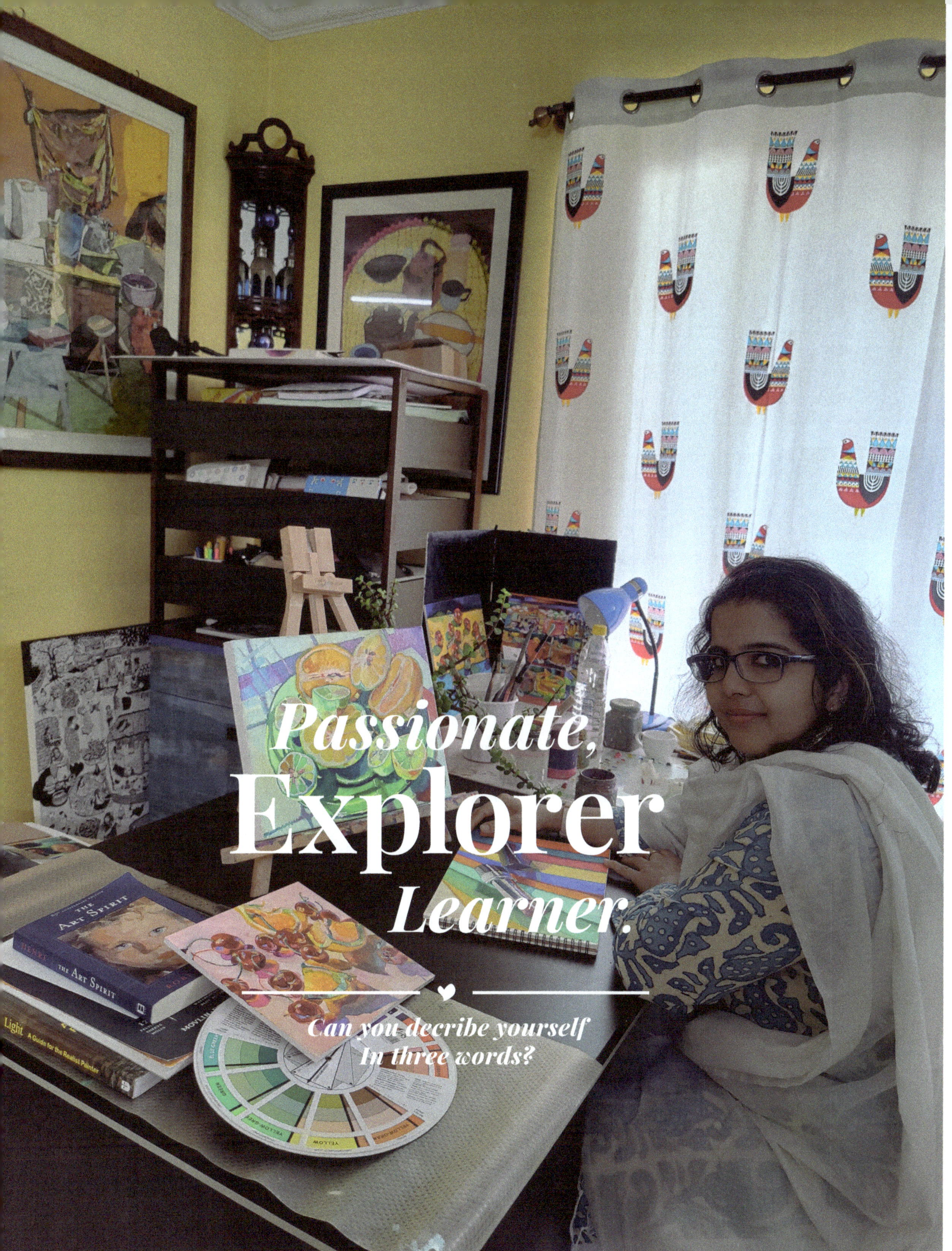

Passionate,
Explorer
Learner.

Can you decribe yourself
In three words?

"Never stop dreaming the impossible."

Fatema is a Bangalore based Fine Artist specialising in oil painting. Primarily self trained, she was born and raised in Kolkata, India, attending school at Loreto Day, Bowbazar and later graduating from Loreto College and thereafter doing a year diploma in Commercial Arts from the Academy of fine arts Kolkata.

In 2018 after a sabbatical of eight long years the creative craving took over and she got back to painting only to find her skills rusted. Determined as always to regain her skills, she began painting everyday and also got selected to participate in Karnataka Chitra Santhe (annually held street fair in Bangalore) from 2019 to 2022.

SO, TELL US ABOUT THE WORK YOU MAKE & WHY?

Becoming a mother and beginning my art practise after a hiatus of eight years my, art now revolves around my home and my surroundings. I discovered magic in the mundane wherein my paintings aim to captivate the beauty and intricacy of everyday objects and experiences.

While I enjoy painting daily scenes of interiors and nature, still life is an important component of my art practice. They allow me the dramatic play of light and shadow and use of expressive and bold brushwork. I love painting loosely with accuracy to drawing yet maintaining a certain liveliness with the use of vibrant and bright colors.

I am always excited to paint a plate of sliced fruits, a pile of books, a loaf of bread or a cup of tea and find different color combinations and arrangements to make the same subject look interesting every time.

Painting various kind of surfaces like metal, glass, ceramic and how they reflect light and the objects around them offers me challenges to explore and stretch my artistic abilities even more.

WHERE DO YOU FIND YOUR PURPOSE AS AN ARTIST?

Art is my purpose to live. As a child who was always low on self confidence and shy, creativity and painting were my tools to expressive myself boldly and fearlessly.My determination and passion saw me through a rough period when I failed the entrance test to get through art school. My failure motivated me to work harder to achieve my goal of becoming an artist without any formal art education.

Two turning points redefined my purpose as an artist. Firstly the myth that you can become an artist only by a certain age and by getting an art school education.

And secondly, I believe that art is a skill which can be learned at any age and stage in life.

I restarted my art practice again at the age of thirty eight and I feel now I am even more clear as to what and where I want to go with my art. As an artist I want show my work at any possible opportunity I get and I want to make my paintings affordable and accessible to all.

I feel that owning or buying a piece of original art shouldn't be a privilege but a necessity to make homes and spaces more beautiful. Painting is not only restricted to making realistic drawings ,there is no 'only one possible way' to paint an object.

WHAT WOULD YOU DO WITH YOUR ART, IF YOU HAD NO FEAR?

With no fear I would definitely fulfill my dream of studying figurative painting at any traditional art ateliers in Europe and then go on to paint human forms freely in every posture possible on every street wall in the world!

Show my paintings without any fear at all the big art biennales and prestigious art galleries of the world and have my published in renowned art & design magazines. Travel the world and paint everywhere without the fear of being judged.

IF YOU HAVE THE WORLD'S ATTENTION FOR 30 SECONDS, WHAT IS THAT YOU WOULD LIKE TO SAY?

Never stop dreaming the impossible. Never let others' opinions affect your passion and determination. I strongly believe that bloom where you are planted and spread your roots from there. Paint regularly and paint small. Make lots of bad art, because always remember, a failed effort means you found another way of painting which didn't work and there are still a thousand more ways to explore!

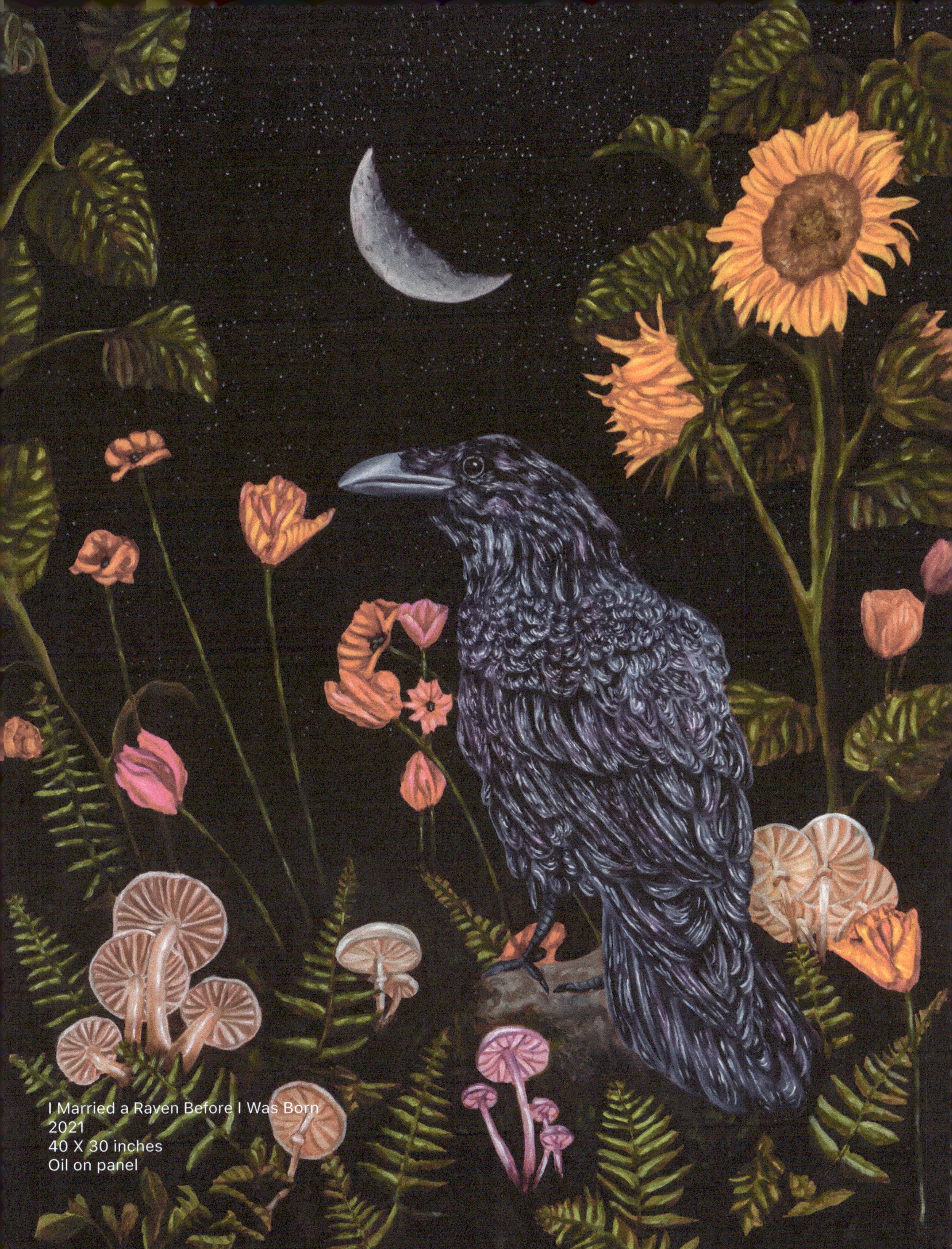

I Married a Raven Before I Was Born
2021
40 X 30 inches
Oil on panel

Elisa Vita

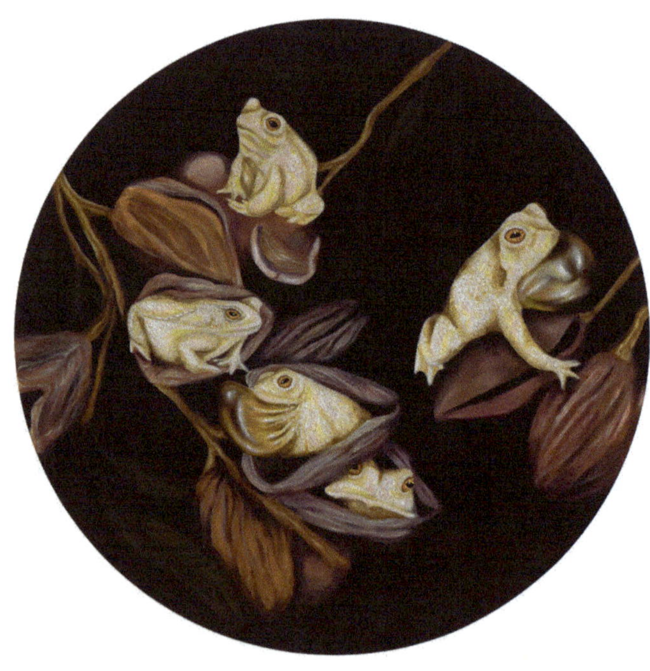

Elisa Vita is a Canadian artist. Her approach to paintings is *narrative* and *poetic*. She hopes for her artwork o serve as a *visual portal* for viewers.

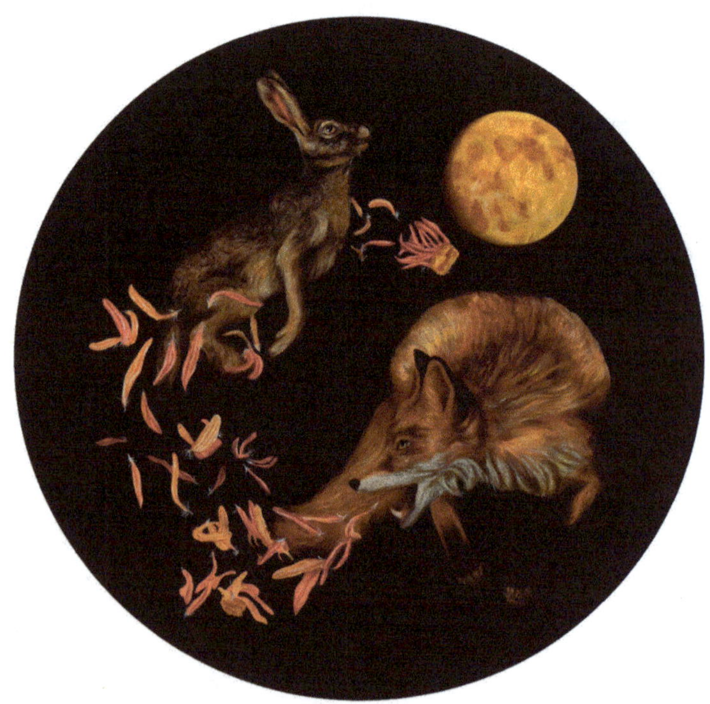

Feasting in a Famine
2020
30 X 30 inches
Oil on panel

https://elisavita.com
@elisavitafineart

From the Devil's Mouth
2020
30 X 30 inches
Oil on panel

Passionate,
Persistant,
Curious.

Can you decribe yourself
In three words?

My purpose as an artist comes from the need to find beauty in dark places, to hold space for intense wonder and grief simultaneously.

I think fear is an important part of my process. Art making allows me to alchemize fear and anxiety into something new and more hopeful, so I truly cannot imagine what imagery I would generate without it.

Maybe we should all be a little kinder to each other.

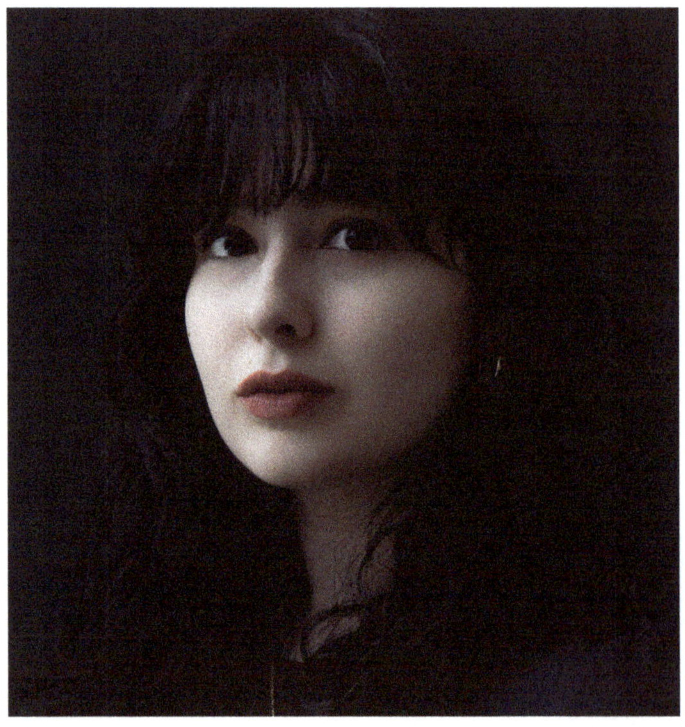

"Maybe we should all be a little kinder to each other."

Elisa Vita is a Canadian artist. She holds a BFA in Painting and Drawing from Concordia University, QC, and is currently pursuing an MFA in Visual Arts at York University, ON. Her approach to painting is narrative and poetic. She hopes for her artwork to serve as a visual portal for viewers, coaxing them deeper into their internal worlds, and reminding them of the magic therein.

SO, TELL US ABOUT THE WORK YOU MAKE & WHY?
My artistic curiosity lies in the cyclical patterns of the natural world. I am particularly enchanted with the liminal spaces which emerge when the peak of vibrancy declines into decay. My approach to these transitional spaces is corporal. My body, through the process of painting, acts as a permeable membrane through which the environment is transmuted. During this time, flora and fauna shape-shift into the inhabitants of personal mythologies and fables.

I use wandering as a methodology for art making, drawing parallels between the act of meandering across a panel and through the woods. My process intimately draws from reference imagery collected during my woodland walks, as well as my own experiences interacting with the non-human. Previously, the non-human beings which I primarily collaborate with: raven, hare, owl, and fox, have been uprooted from any discernible environment and reframed against the flat, black backgrounds of my panels. This black space is a psychological one as well as a spiritual one.Within it, their stories unfold. As my practice develops, I am exploring the potential of the forest itself to act as a psychological and mythological space.

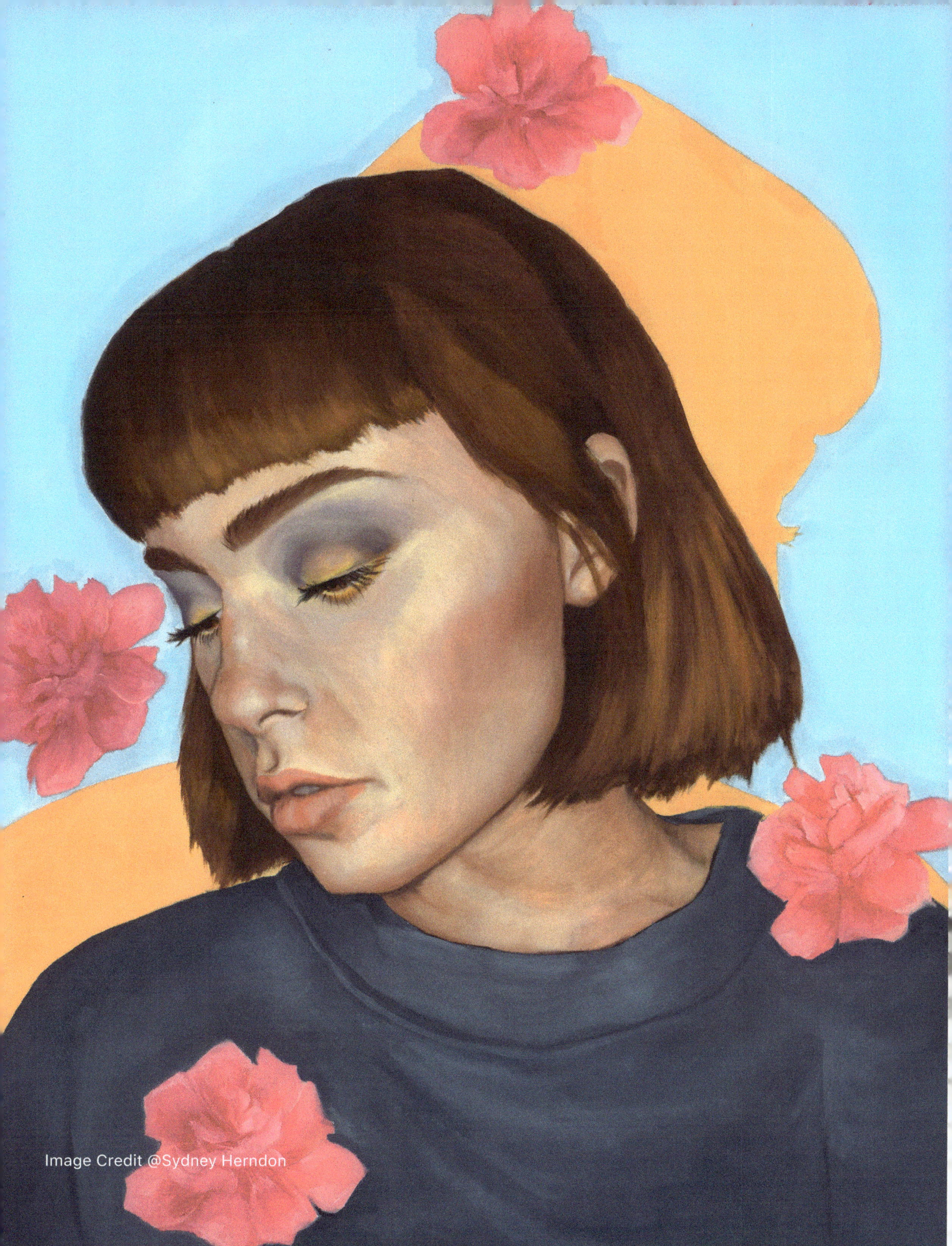
Image Credit @Sydney Herndoh

Sydney Herndon

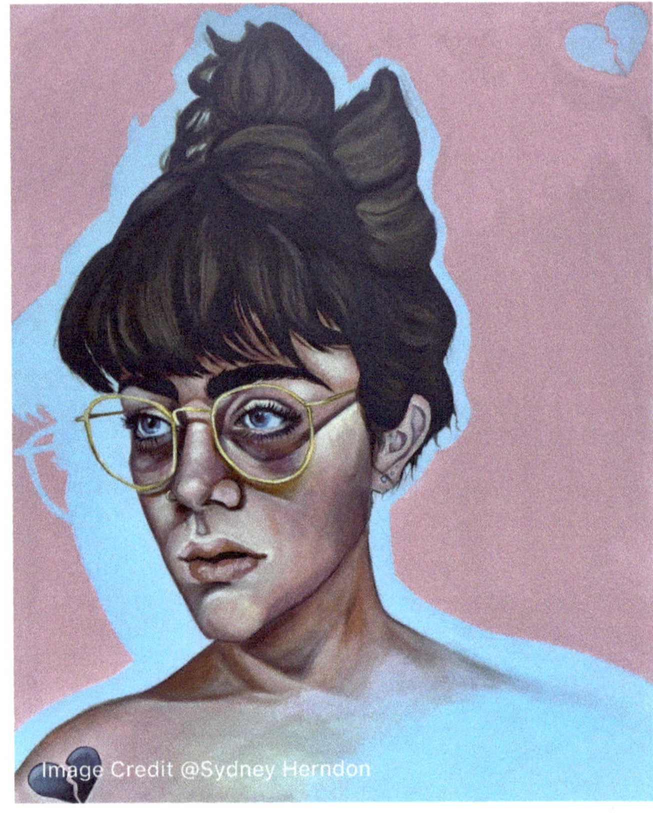

www.sydneyherndon.com
@sydneymarieh

Sydney Herndon from Russellville, Kentucky, focuses on *millennial women* and *symbology* that allows the viewer a glimpse into the *mental worlds of the paintings.*

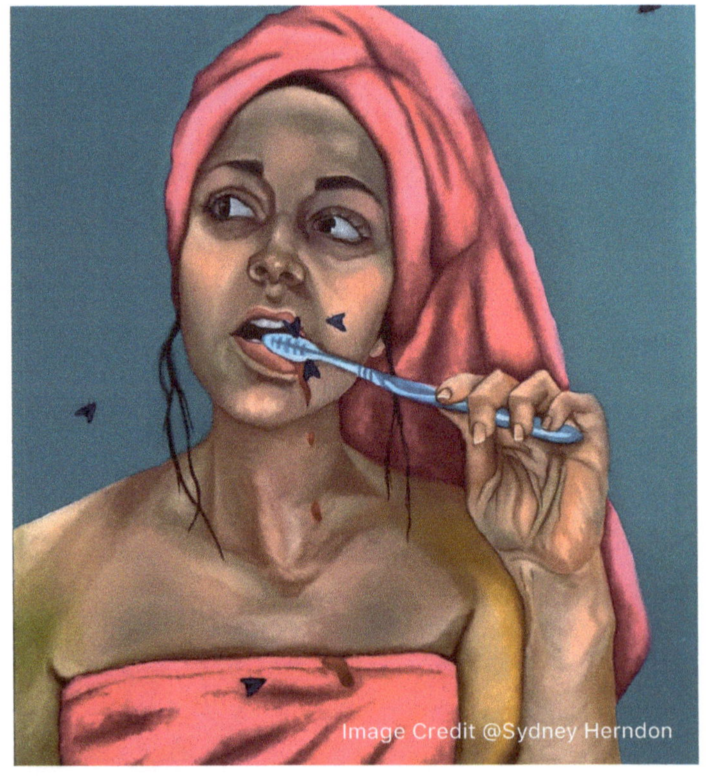

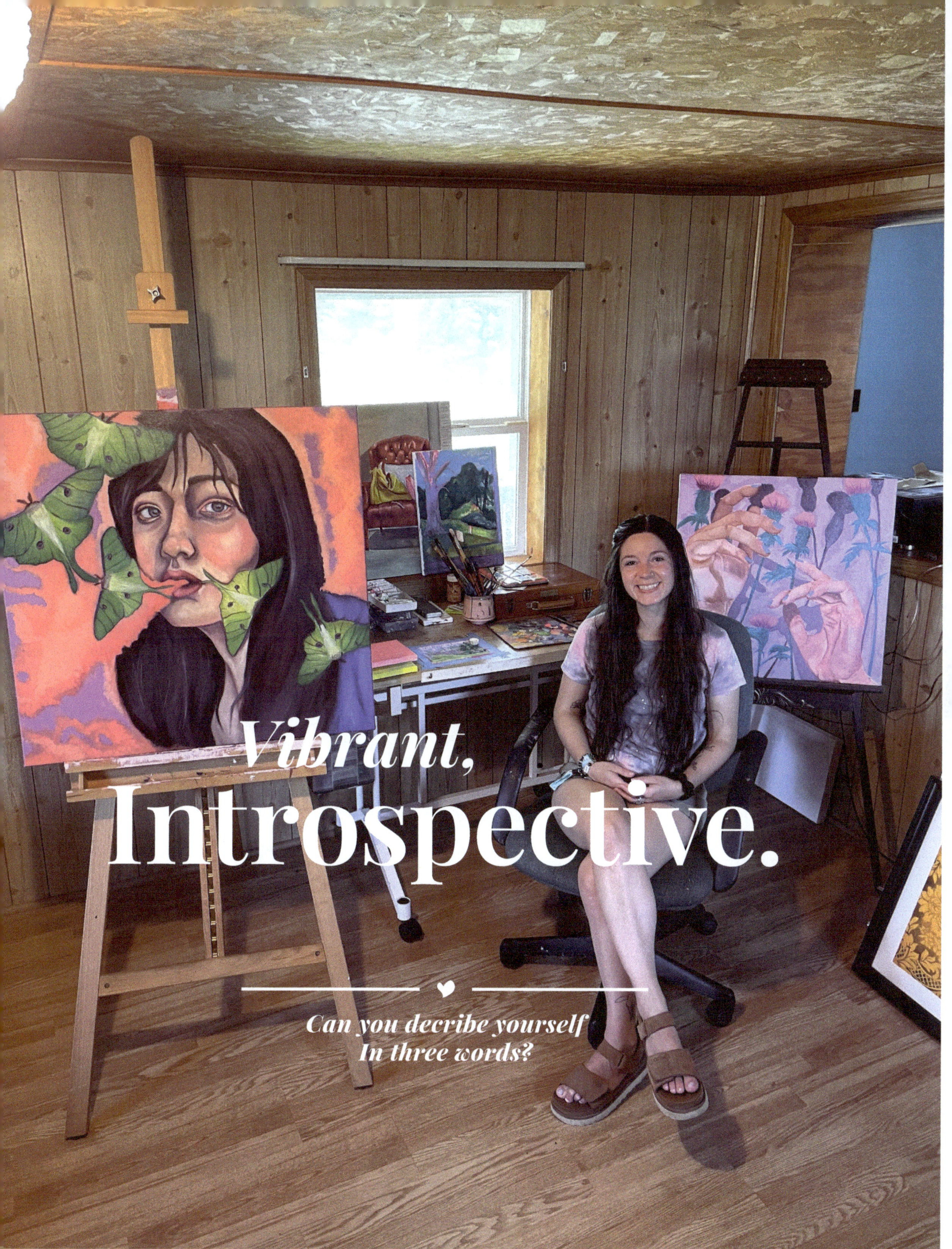

Vibrant,
Introspective.

Can you decribe yourself
In three words?

Sydney Herndon was born in Russellville, Kentucky. In 2018 she graduated from Western Kentucky University where she was awarded a Bachelor of Fine Arts in Painting, and a Bachelor of Arts in Ceramics. Sydney's work has been included in art magazines such as, Pikchur Magazine, Candyfloss Magazine, and We are Zanna, a London based contemporary art magazine. Her work has been included in The Women in the Arts Exhibit in New York City and the 2019 Art Juxtaposed Exhibit in Rosendale, New York. Sydney focuses primarily on painting using both traditional oil paint and digital painting techniques. Her work focuses on millennial women and symbology that allows the viewer a glimpse into the mental worlds of the paintings.

SO, TELL US ABOUT THE WORK YOU MAKE & WHY?

Using symbols and bright colors in contrast with traditional portraiture, my work explores the various mental states of women in today's society. The portraits rely on the imposition of specific symbols and the unease of heightened color to convey what the subject is actually feeling. Because my art practice is a direct response to my own internalized feelings, I explore the pressures that women face in their day-to-day lives to hide their negative emotions behind some kind of an exterior. For me an idea comes from songs, images, mythology and moments in everyday life that connect with our modern world. I begin by making connections to my ongoing theme, then, research what symbols or motifs would fit a specific image. In my painting, Get Clean, flies buzz around a young woman brushing her teeth. These flies represent the anxiety, depression and worry that can cloud our normal everyday routines and make the smallest tasks more than we can handle. The bright colors are used in contrast to the symbols as a way of "hiding" the negative emotions. I present symbols such as moths, flies, rats, etc. over the figure to allude to the depression, anxiety, and mental health issues that run through our minds on a daily basis. Some of the figures in my paintings have healed from these issues or are in a state of healing. In my painting, Perfect Spaces, flowers represent a perfect internalized world: a place the mind can go, free of these negative thoughts.

WHERE DO YOU FIND YOUR PURPOSE AS AN ARTIST?

I find my purpose as an artist by looking to the natural world for inspiration and making connections to human feelings and consciousness.

I get inspired by the rare and bright colors found in nature that some would consider "unnatural."

WHAT WOULD YOU DO WITH YOUR ART, IF YOU HAD NO FEAR?

If I had no fear I would I would create more art without restrictions placed on me by myself and society. I would create without the fear of judgment surrounding my themes and ideas. If I had no fear I would not water down my ideas for fear of what the masses may think.

IF YOU HAVE THE WORLD'S ATTENTION FOR 30 SECONDS, WHAT IS THAT YOU WOULD LIKE TO SAY?

Because of Covid I think we've all had a lot of time for introspection and know we as a society cannot continue to live how we have. Through community building, arts, education and togetherness we can be and build the change we want to see in the world.

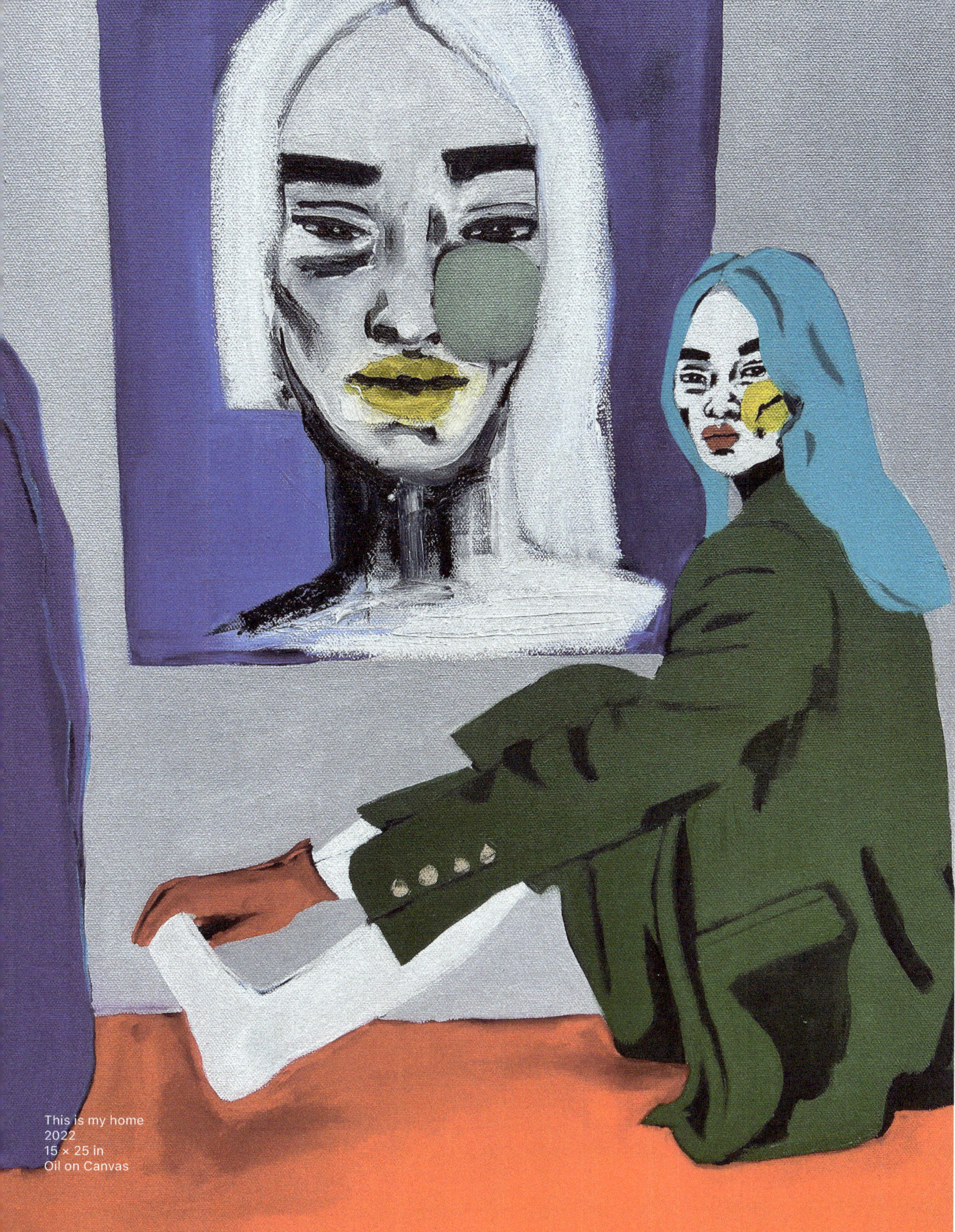

This is my home
2022
15 × 25 in
Oil on Canvas

Ana Sneeringer

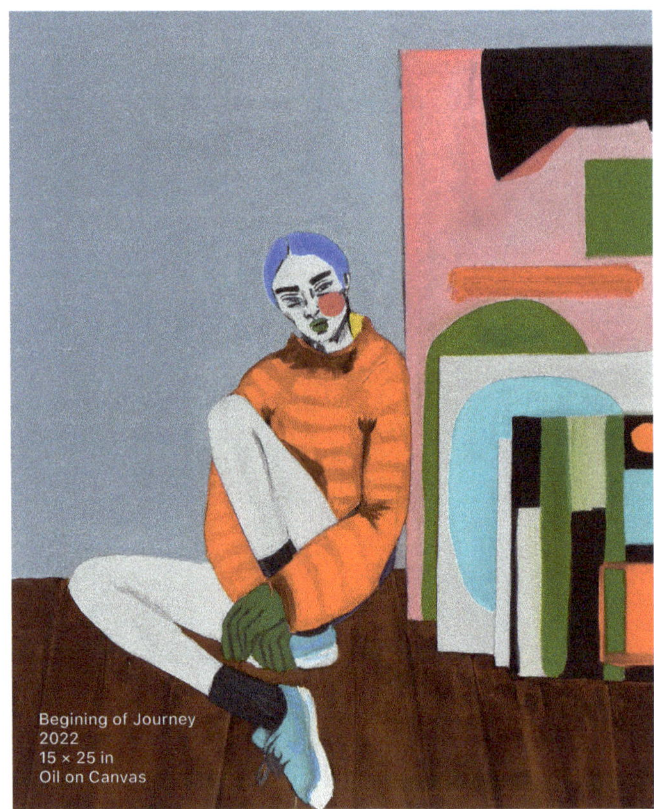

https://anasneeringer.com

@ana_sneeringer

Ana Sneeringer is a Slovenian artist. Her artistic canvas is a *vivid, kleidoscopic world of thoughts, emotions* and *experiences* shared by the *modern woman.*

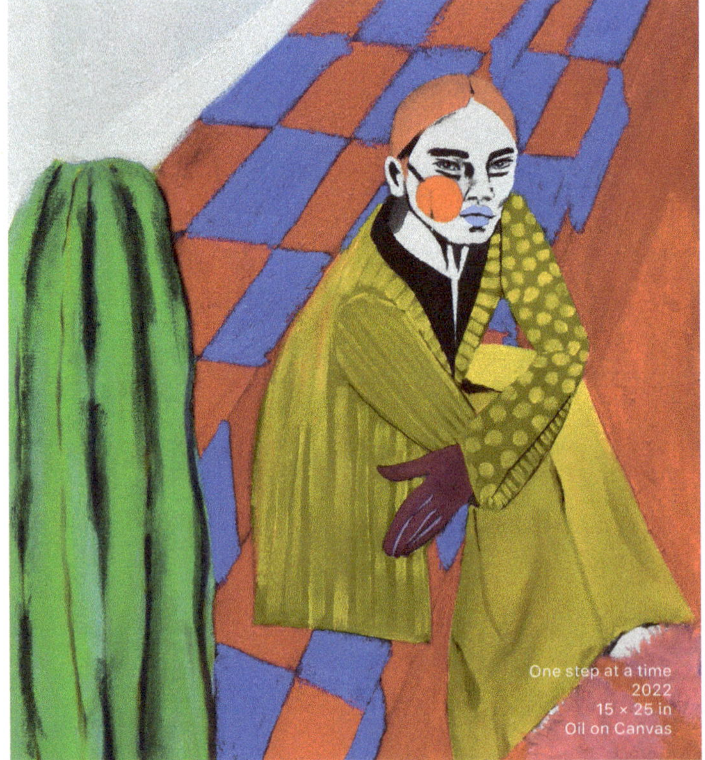

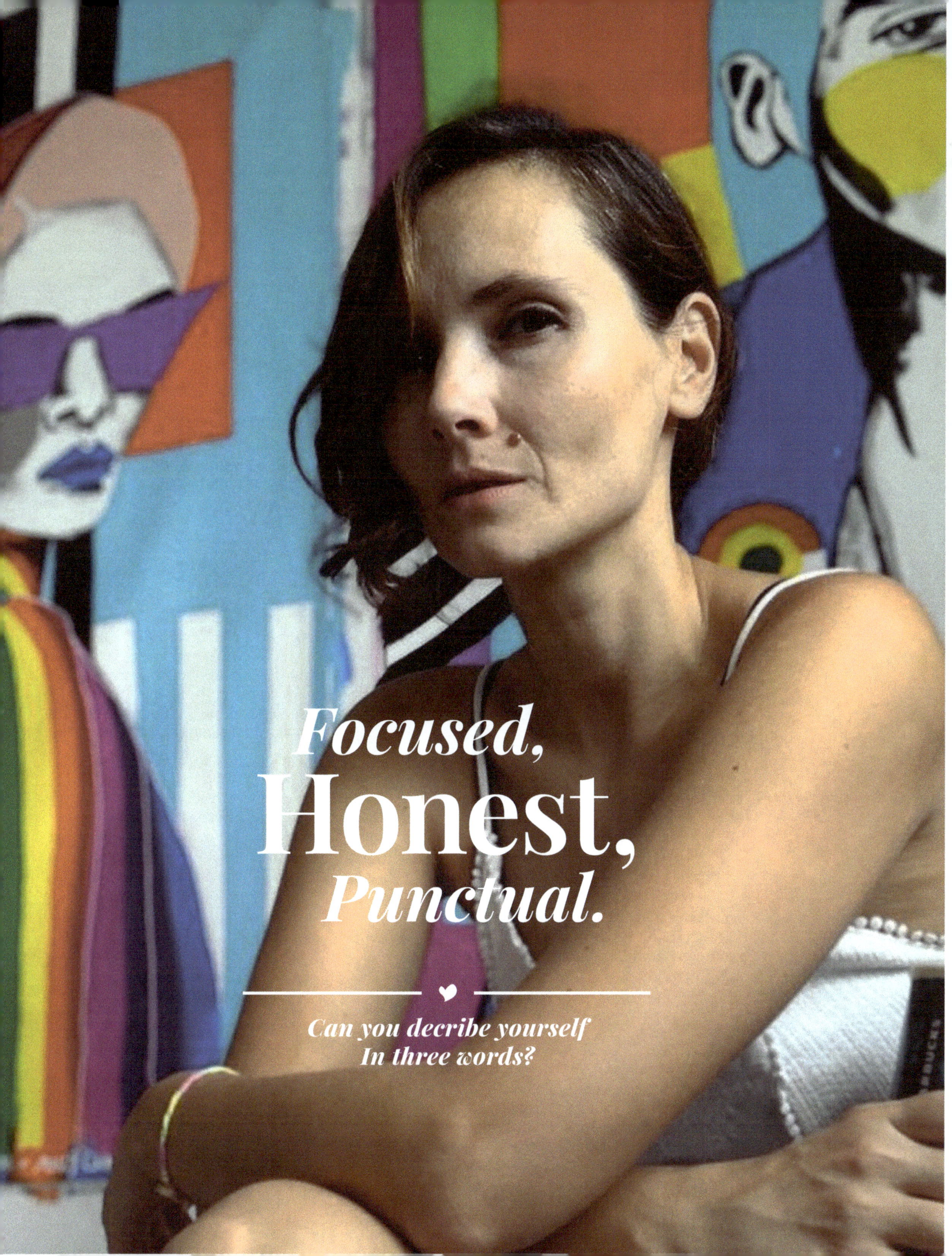

Focused,
Honest,
Punctual.

Can you decribe yourself
In three words?

"To never be someone else but yourself!"

Ana Sneeringer is a Slovenian artist residing in Montgomery, AL, USA. Having started her career in documentary journalism as a director of an environmental television station, Ana's experiences across, France, Jordan, Russia, the USA, The Dominican Republic, The Netherlands, and India, led her to express her observations & learnings in her contemporary artworks. Women or the female presence form the epicenter of her artistic exploration and stories. Living around the world and engaging with women from different cultures, Ana's encounters resonated with the similarities of emotions and experiences everywhere, rather than the disparities of race or color. As a result, her artistic canvas is a vivid, kaleidoscopic world of thoughts, emotions, and experiences shared by the modern woman. Entirely self-taught, Ana finds liberation in employing free will and speaking from her heart, unconfined by a learned discipline. Whether in watercolor, acrylic, or digital media, she gives herself the freedom to experiment based on her subject matter.

Ana's art has been exhibited internationally in the United Arab Emirates, Italy, the United States, the United Kingdom, Canada, India, and Switzerland. All She Makes, Create! Magazine and Beautiful Bizarre Magazine, highly recognizable art platforms for contemporary artists of the 21st century, and World of Interiors, the most influential design and decoration magazine from Conde Nast, featured her work. She had been interviewed by Adobe2 and many other magazines. One of her projects was collaborating with LIDL Slovenia and Europa Donna to raise breast cancer awareness through her artwork. In 2020 one of her artworks was exhibited and is now part of their collection in one of three National museums in India, Salar Jung Museum, Hyderabad, India.

SO, TELL US ABOUT THE WORK YOU MAKE & WHY?

My art practice is not precisely something I am making up. Instead, it is coming as an inner call to paint my story, and I want to vocalize it through my portraits and figures. My art is about human rights with a woman as a leading depiction. My protagonists are women with strong character and energy who express raw emotions and aren't afraid to show their genuine and natural personalities. Female figures in my art represent quirky and unique ladies of real life, enjoying or learning to enjoy themselves by accepting themselves as unity and converting this realization into the superior power of proudness and achievability. We can't run from the daily emotions we face. I need to capture and express these feelings through my work to show the world how strong humans are, especially women.

My work speaks the language of the country I live in at the moment. In April 2022, I moved to the United States, where I am continuing to live an inspiration I've collected that shaped me for over a decade of living in different countries around the world. I am currently focusing on how changes impact women lives who celebrate themselves outside their comfort zone. We all cope great in a comfort zone, but we only stagnate or bloom very slowly in that state. You are left with a blank canvas to paint your new story when you lose your comfort zone. Playing with subjects like cars and plants is my synonym for understanding the speed, durability, and strength one choose to go in life.

WHERE DO YOU FIND YOUR PURPOSE AS AN ARTIST?

I find it everywhere where the art is. But, of course, life itself is a purpose, especially when you meet inspiring people and see their life as a motivator to keep going on. But most of the time, I find my purpose in my studio when I am left alone with my art supplies and thoughts.

WHAT WOULD YOU DO WITH YOUR ART, IF YOU HAD NO FEAR?

I love this question. I, honestly, don't have fear for my art. If you are not authentic in creating your art, you can't be true to your purpose. I create without fear because I don't get bothered if people don't like my art.

IF YOU HAVE THE WORLD'S ATTENTION FOR 30 SECONDS, WHAT IS THAT YOU WOULD LIKE TO SAY?

To never be someone else but yourself!

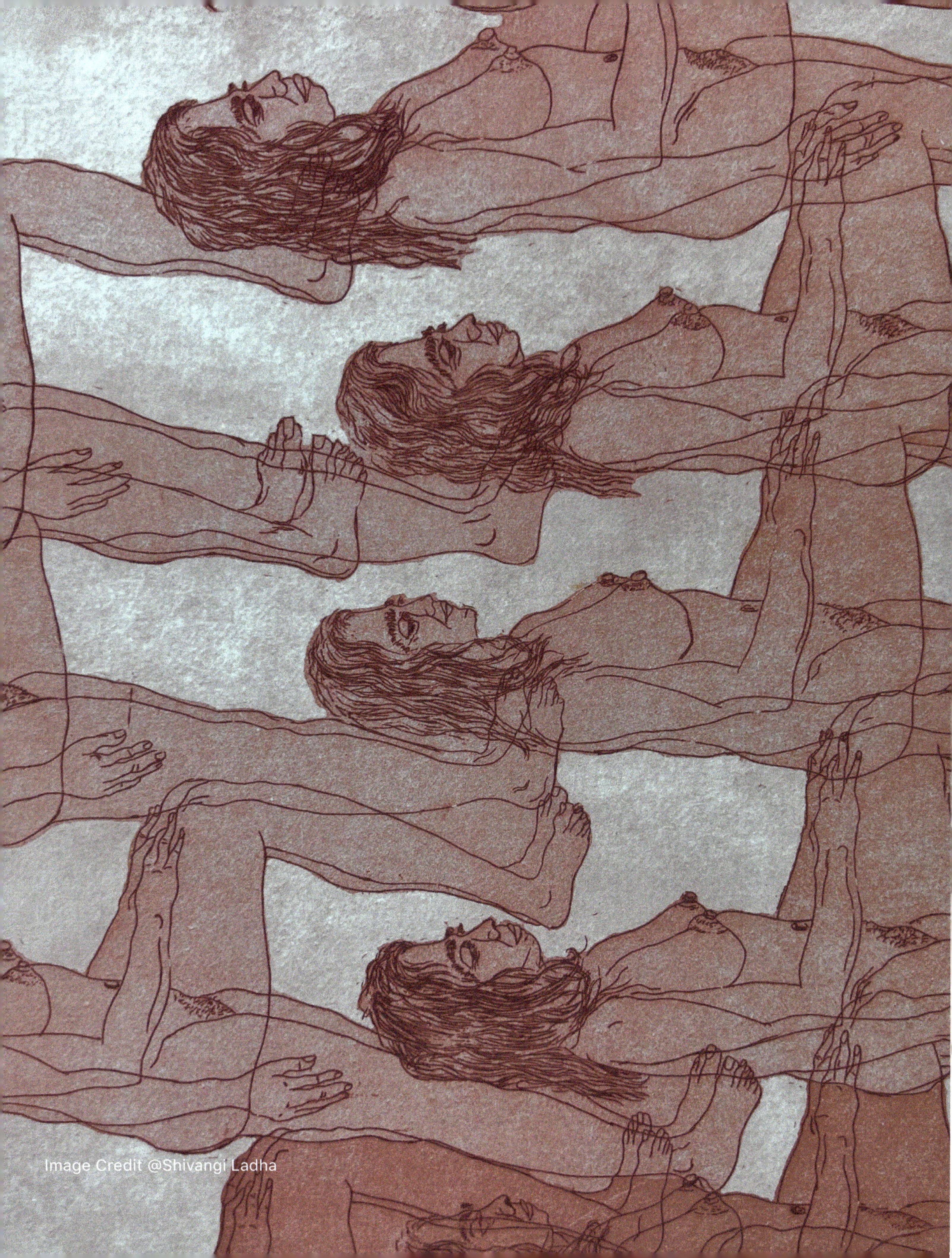

Shivangi Ladha

Shivangi Ladha is an artist from India. Through her work, she likes to *question* the *true identity* of our *beloved human race*.

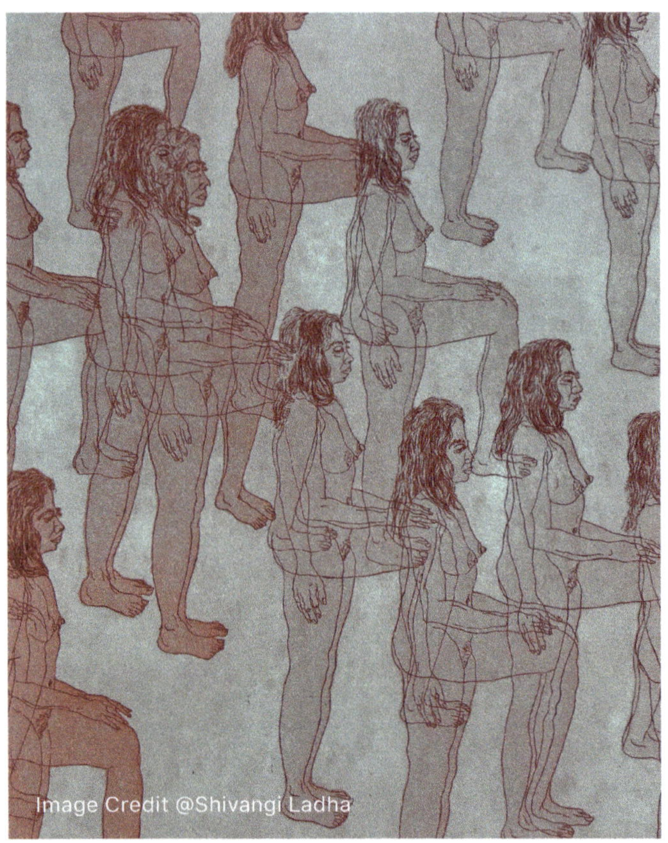

www.shivangiladha.com
@shivangiladhastudio

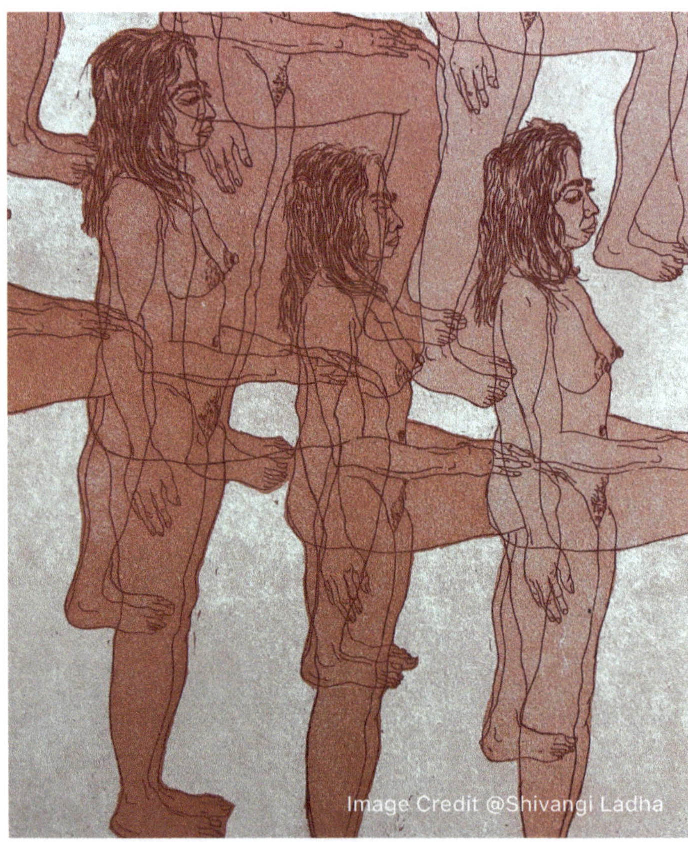

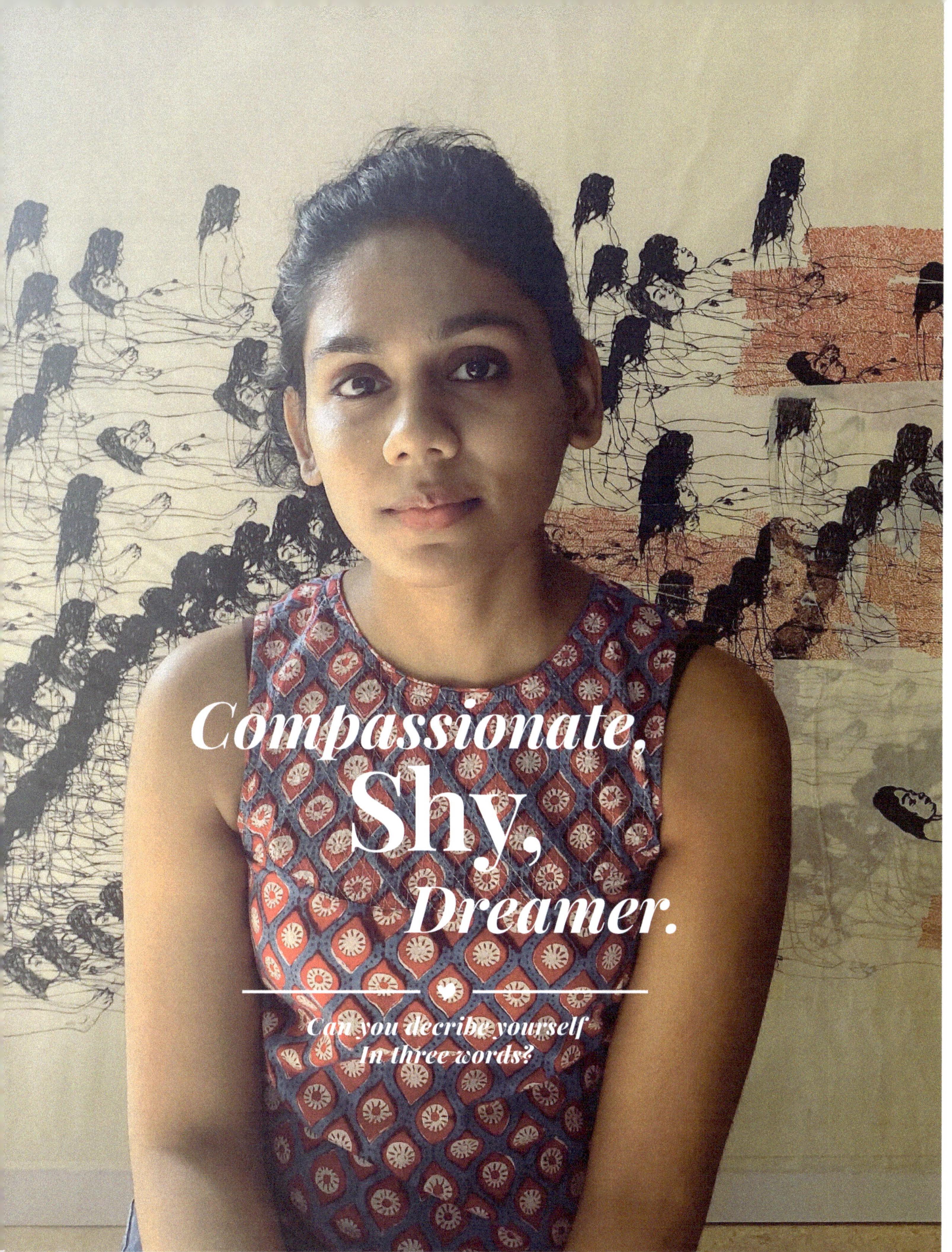

Compassionate,
Shy,
Dreamer.
Can you decribe yourself
In three words?

Shivangi Ladha graduated from Royal College of Art London, in 2016 with MA in Printmaking. Since then she has undertaken several residencies & taught internationally in the UK, Spain, Canada and the USA and consistently exhibited work which has entered prestigious private and public collections such as the Snap Studio, East London Printmakers, Women's Studio Workshop, V&A, the British Museum, Mead Museum, Reliance Foundation, Anant Art Gallery to name a few.

This year she received the award for the TAF emerging artist South Asia, by The Arts Family, London; Global Talent Award by Art Council England and got nominated for the Queen Sonja Print Award, Sweden a major international print prize.

She has also created a space for other artists to show and make work by initiating India Printmaker House, a platform to facilitate workshops, exhibitions, prizes and residencies.

SO, TELL US ABOUT THE WORK YOU MAKE & WHY?
Shivangi Ladha's work questions the true identity of our beloved human race. She uses a self- referential process to channel her engagement with social, political and ecological spaces through the human body. Her print represents the collective voice of a crowd - a crowd seeking to rise and transcend to a place or state where there is no differentiation between gender, sexuality, race, caste, creed, disability and class, where we are essentially all one and the same from within.

WHERE DO YOU FIND YOUR PURPOSE AS AN ARTIST?
The process of creating art excites me. Art makes me ponder upon the deeper questions of life and makes me self reflect. Through it I am able to reconnect with myself, which sometimes I tend to loose in today's lifestyle!

WHAT WOULD YOU DO WITH YOUR ART, IF YOU HAD NO FEAR?
I would scribble on the walls of my Mother's bedroom.

IF YOU HAVE THE WORLD'S ATTENTION FOR 30 SECONDS, WHAT IS THAT YOU WOULD LIKE TO SAY?
That 'you' are boundless, limitless and infinite.

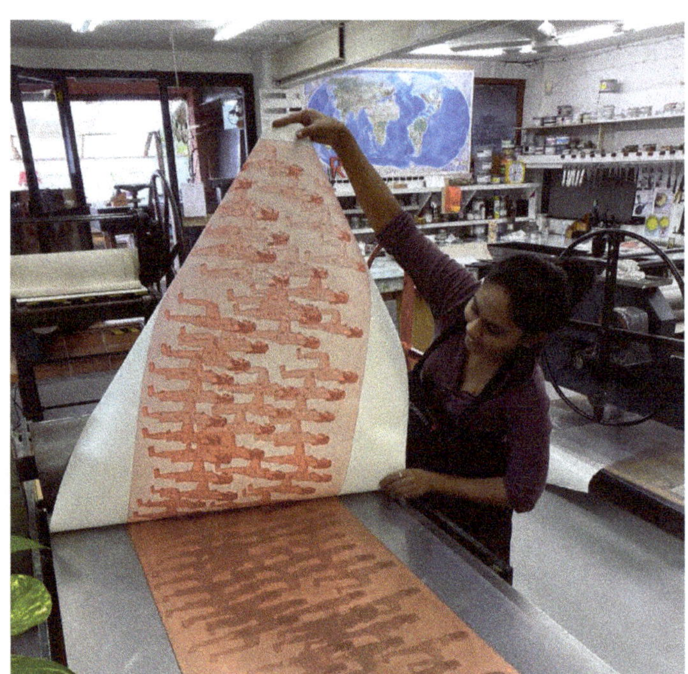

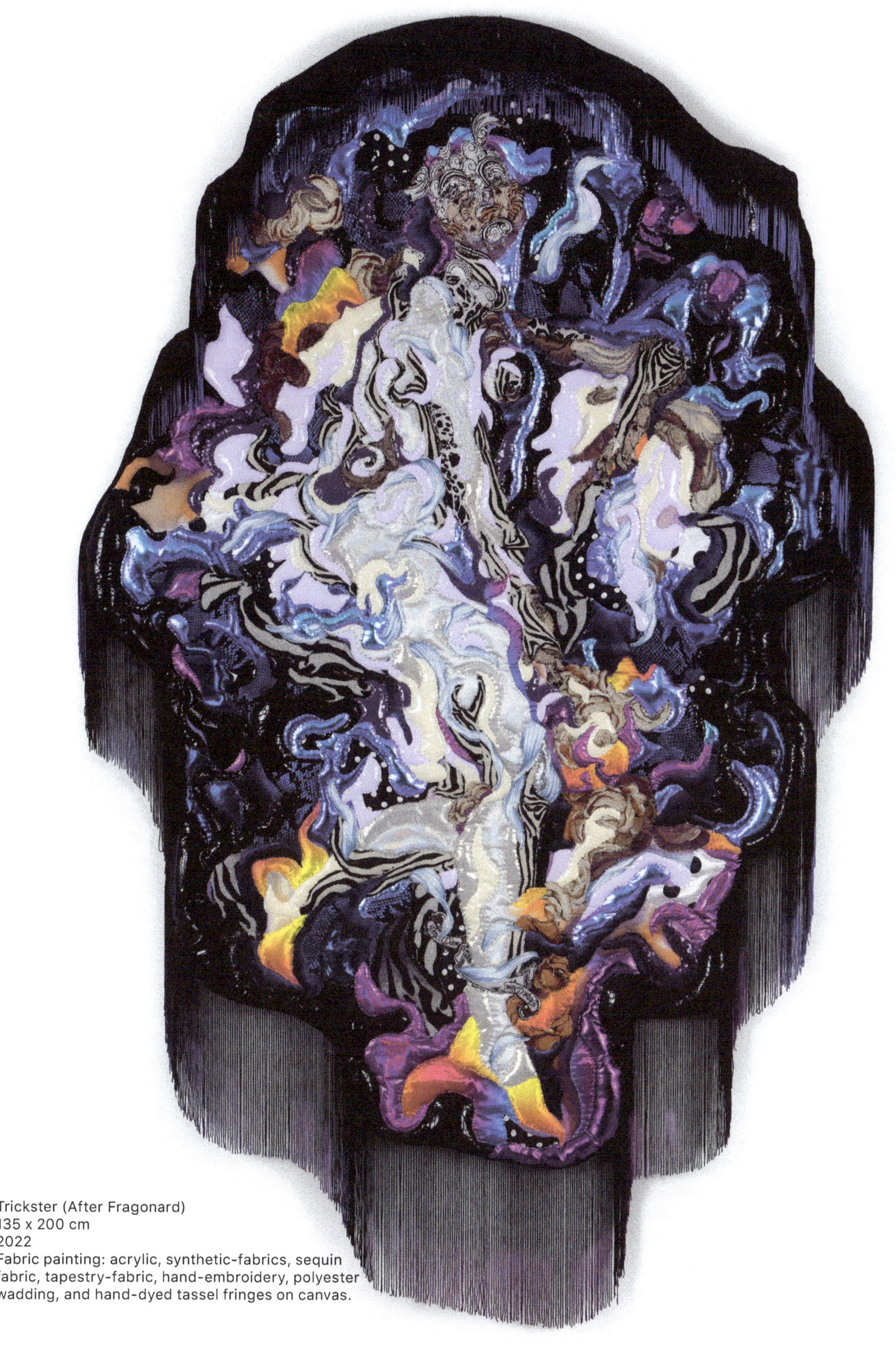

Trickster (After Fragonard)
135 x 200 cm
2022
Fabric painting: acrylic, synthetic-fabrics, sequin fabric, tapestry-fabric, hand-embroidery, polyester wadding, and hand-dyed tassel fringes on canvas.

Anne Von Freyburg

Her practice rethinks *textile* and the *decorative* within the *tradition of painting*. It embraces and subverts the *female gaze*, the *feminine* and pretty.

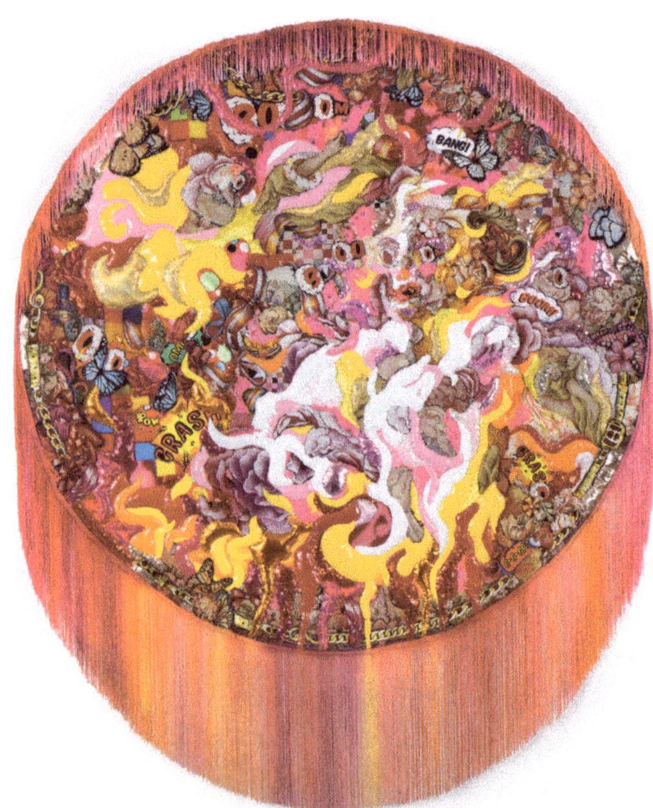

I want Candy (After Fragonard)
110 x 140 cm
2022
Fabric painting: acrylic, synthetic-fabrics, sequin fabric, tapestry-fabric, hand-embroidery, polyester wadding, and hand-dyed tassel fringes on canvas

https://annevonfreyburg.com/

@*annevonfreyburg*

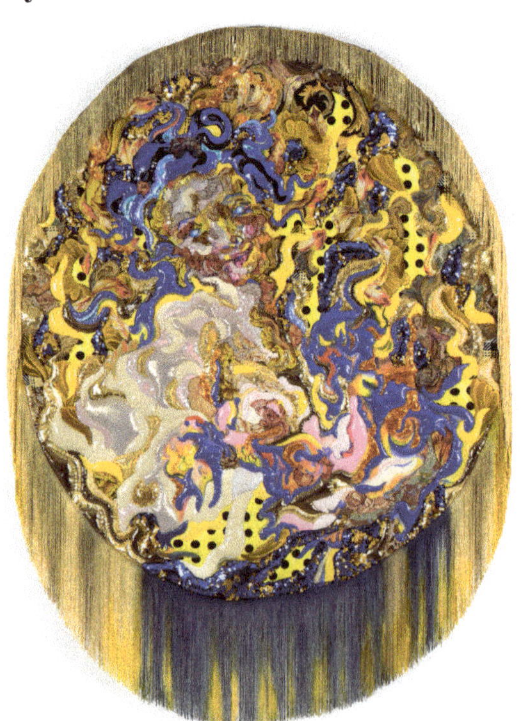

Untitled (after Fragonard)
110 x 160 cm
2021
Fabric painting: acrylic, synthetic-fabrics, spray-paint, tapestry-fabric, hand-embroidery, polyester wadding, and hand-dyed tassel fringes on canvas.

Empathic, Determined, *Playful.*

Untitled (After Fragonard)
185 x 185 cm
2021

Fabric painting: acrylic, synthetic-fabrics, sequin fabric, tapestry-fabric, hand-embroidery, polyester wadding, and hand-dyed tassel fringes on canvas

Image Credit @Barry Macdonald

"Be yourself everyone else is already taken."

Anne von Freyburg (b. 1979) is a Dutch artist based in London. She received her MFA from Goldsmiths (2016) and holds a BA in Fashion Design from ArtEZ Arnhem, The Netherlands. Her work is part of the Tapestry Triennial at the Central Textile Museum in Lodz, Poland (2022) one of the most prominent international Textile Museums worldwide. Von Freyburg is the winner of Robert Walters UK New Artists Award (2021) and exhibited at Saatchi Gallery, London. She was nominated for The Ingram Prize (2021) and took part in the PLOP x Cob. Winter Residency followed by an exhibition in November (2021). Von Freyburg's work is in several private collections all over the world. The large-scale textile paintings are reconstructed Rococo portraits made out of a mixture of tapestry and contemporary fashion fabrics.

The imagery focuses on a stylised idea around feminine beauty as found in the tradition of Boucher and Fragonard. With these works von Freyburg attempts to raise questions about taste, femininity, high and low art and the constructs of female identity.

SO, TELL US ABOUT THE WORK YOU MAKE & WHY?

The idea of the Rococo portrait translated into fashion fabrics is a reference to a culture obsessed by image, the body and appearance. The work is a nod to the idea of constructed beauty-both in technique as well as in ideology. I see the Rococo portraits as the selfies of their time. Like selfies they portray a constructed and a performed form of femininity and beauty. The puffy effect is a reference to the use of steroids in bodybuilding or cosmetic fillers.

At the same time we live in a time where we look at images on our screen most of the time. Materiality and the sense of touch has become more apparent and desired in an age dominated by digital devices. By creating bodily and haptic paintings made out of various fabrics I wanted to give expression to this lack of touch as well.

Even though the idea behind the work is critical about consumerism and beautification, it can also be read as a celebration of the feminine, the tactile, performance and being who and whatever you would like to be. Acceptance of the unfamiliar and respect and tolerance for individuality should be the way forward.

WHERE DO YOU FIND YOUR PURPOSE AS AN ARTIST?

I am driven by the desire of creating work that rubs against ideas of what is considered to be good taste in art. It is fuelled by my intention to lift the hierarchy between fine art and applied art.

Next to that I aim to stretch and challenge my own tastes and ideas about aesthetics in a fearless and uncompromising way.

If I succeed in uplifting people with my work, make them giggle or inspire them to be bold and creative as well I think I reached my purpose as an artist.

WHAT WOULD YOU DO WITH YOUR ART, IF YOU HAD NO FEAR?

Before I go to the studio I leave 'fear' at home. I want to feel excited when starting a new piece.

Besides that, when working with textiles within a contemporary context one has to be fearless in the first place. Also I always dare myself to be bolder in my work than the last time. This way I keep my work fresh and more interesting to make.

I want to challenge myself and be surprised by my work and hopefully it will have a similar effect on my audience.

IF YOU HAVE THE WORLD'S ATTENTION FOR 30 SECONDS, WHAT IS THAT YOU WOULD LIKE TO SAY?

Be yourself everyone else is already taken.

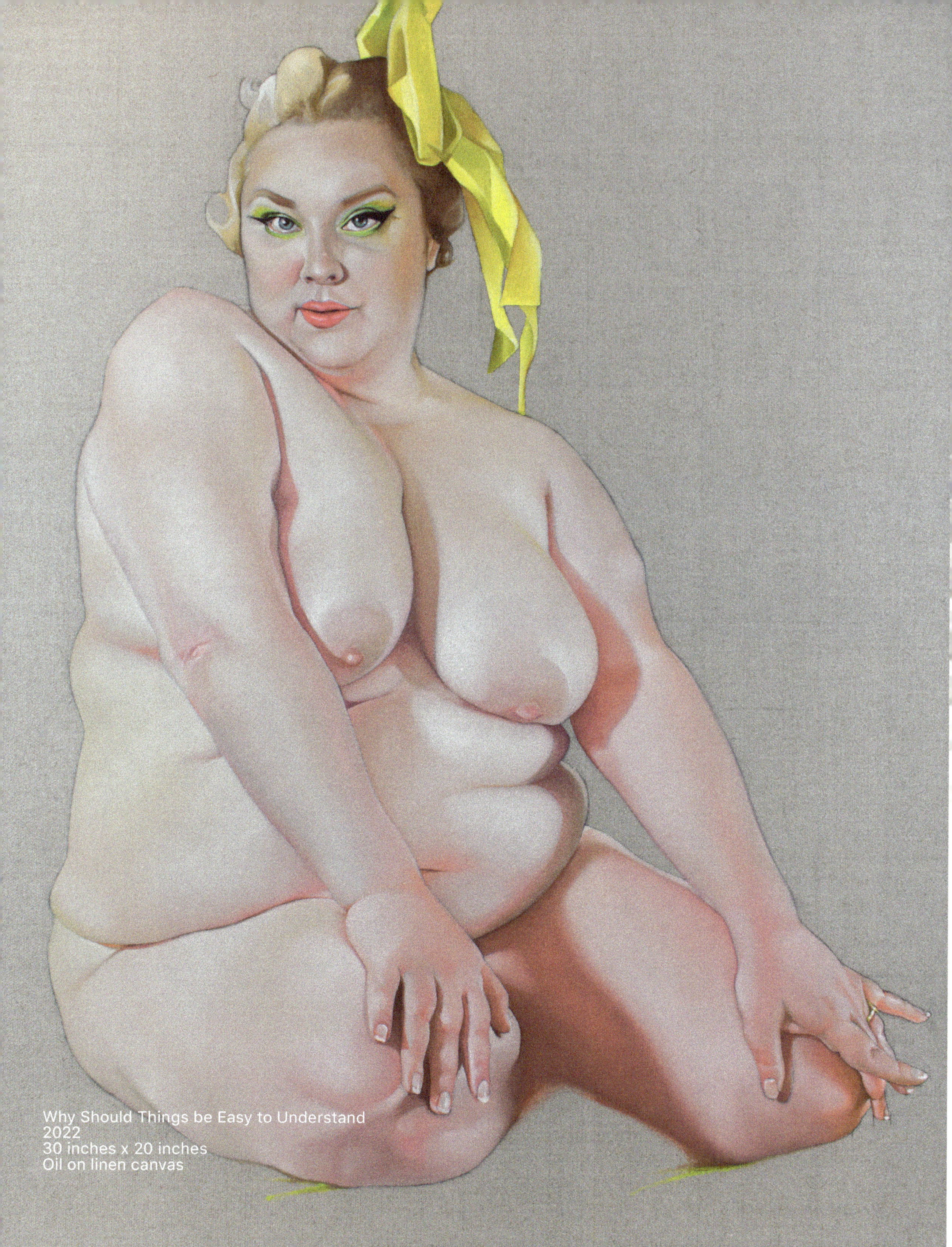
Why Should Things be Easy to Understand
2022
30 inches x 20 inches
Oil on linen canvas

Karen Turner

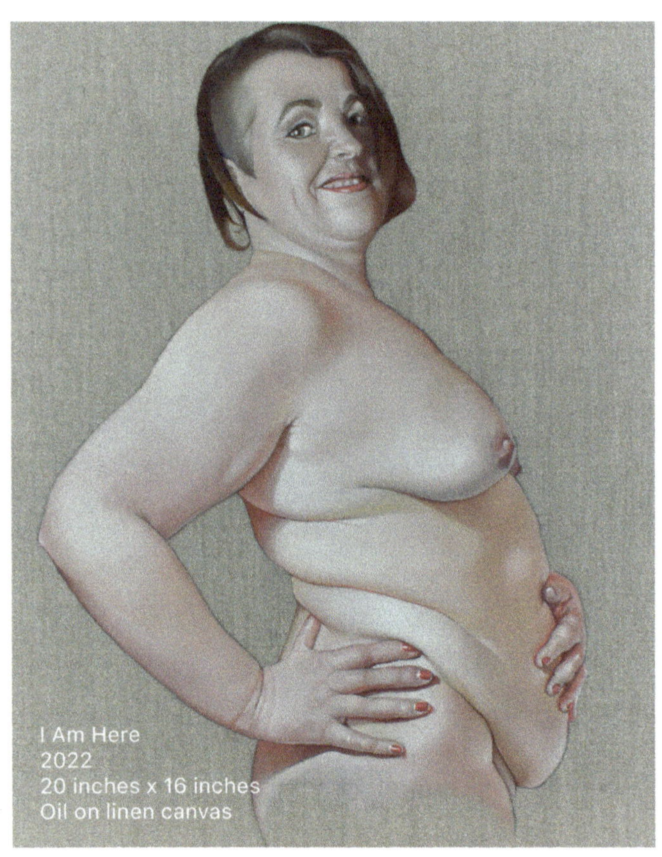

www.karenturnerfineart.com

@karen_turner-artist

Born in London in 1978, Karen is an *award-winning figure artist* whose oil paintings are a *commentary* on the *weight of expectations.*

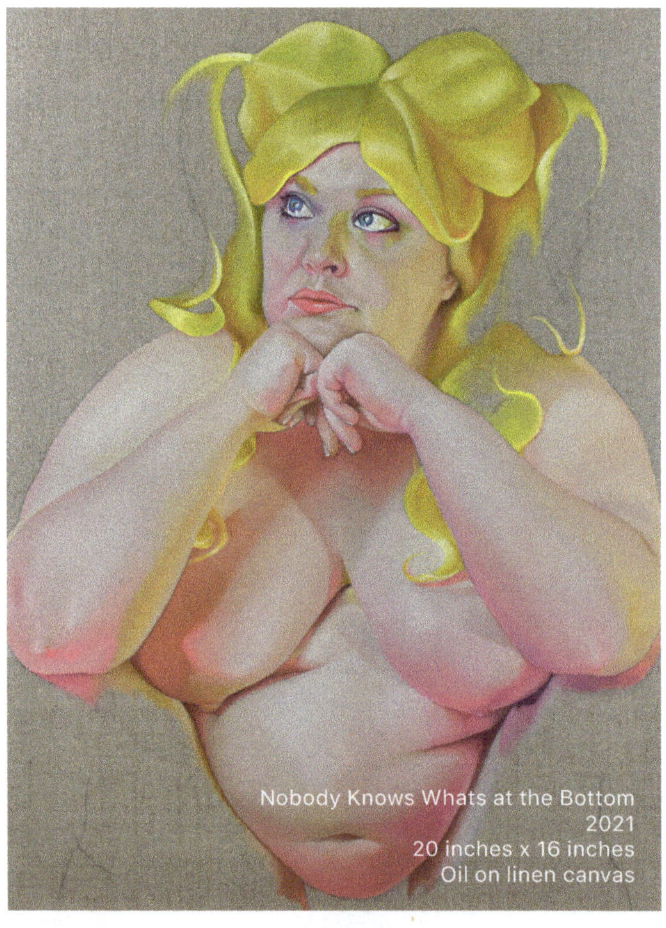

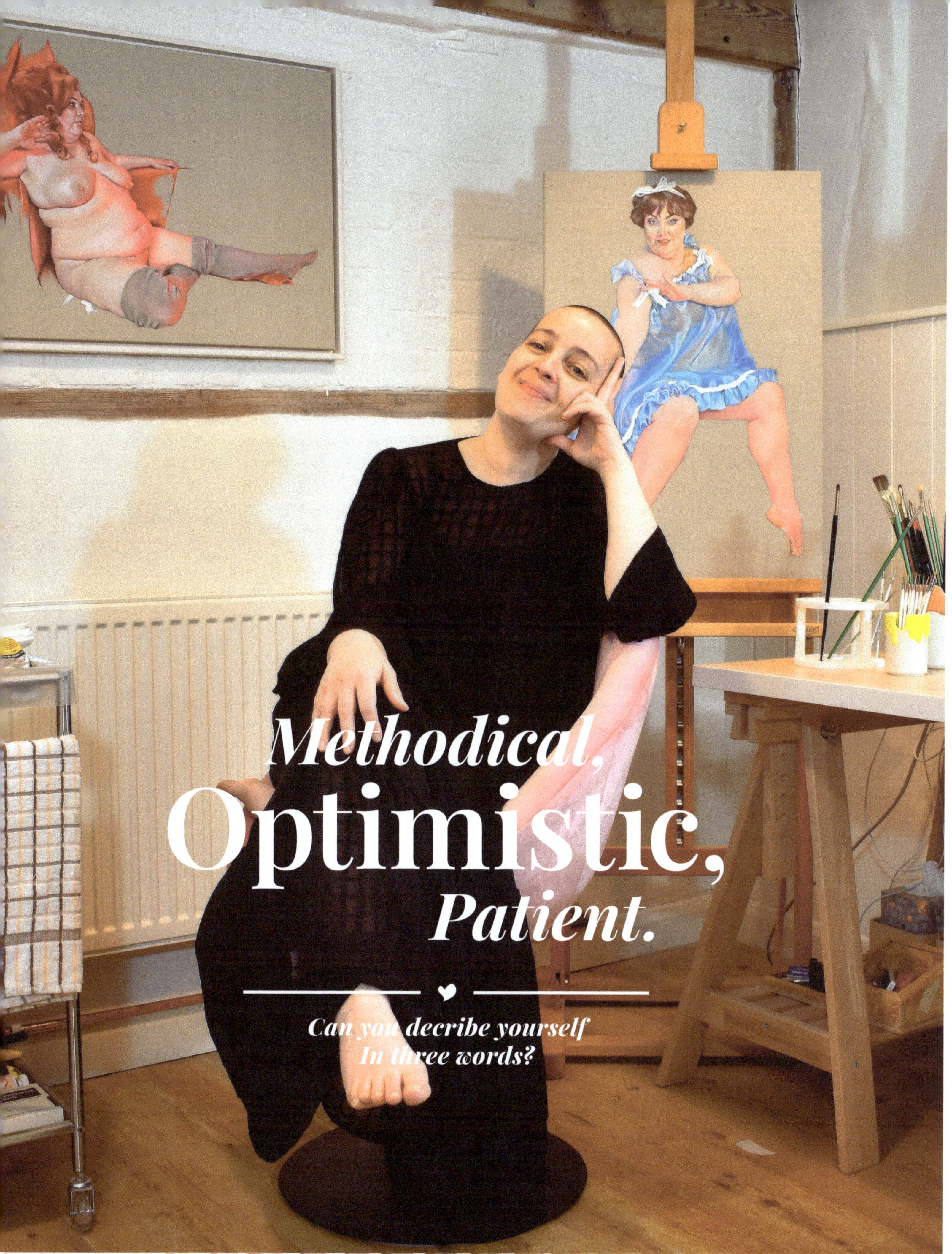

Methodical,
Optimistic,
Patient.
Can you decribe yourself
In three words?

"Stop judging people!"

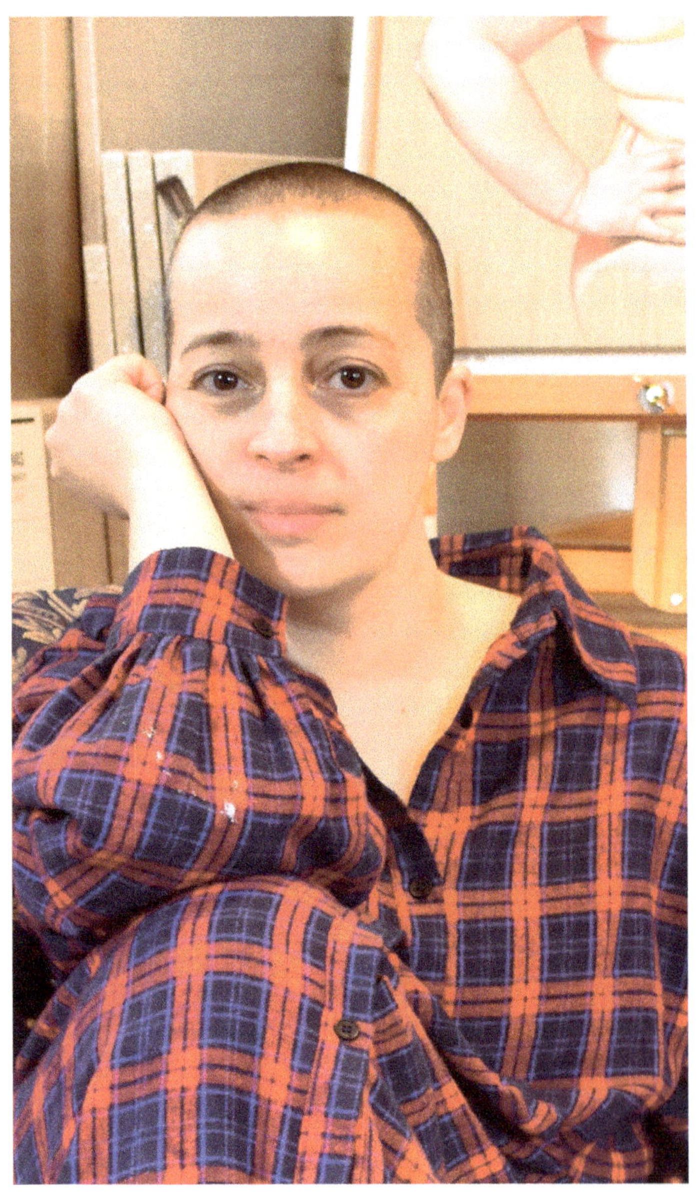

Karen is an award-winning figure artist whose oil paintings are a commentary on the weight of expectations. In 2021 Karen was awarded the President's Prize by the Institute of East Anglian Artists. She was a finalist in the Holly Bush Emerging Woman Painter Prize 2021 and has been shortlisted for the New Emergence Art Prize 2022, the Holly Bush Emerging Woman Painter Prize 2022 and the Women United Art Prize 2021.

SO, TELL US ABOUT THE WORK YOU MAKE & WHY?
With a particular focus on the physical body and the scrutiny to which is it commonly subjected, my paintings explore what society expects of a woman, the ways in which her physical shape is often considered to define her, and the impact that this has on her life and sense of self.

WHERE DO YOU FIND YOUR PURPOSE AS AN ARTIST?

I think what drives me the most is a desire to challenge society's attitudes towards fat bodies. Anti-fat bias is everywhere, and it's particularly extreme when it comes to women. We should be celebrating these fleshy marvels, not shunning them!

WHAT WOULD YOU DO WITH YOUR ART, IF YOU HAD NO FEAR?
I'm not sure that I do have any fear when it comes to my art. The fear probably comes from everything surrounding the art - when do you give up the day job, for example? But even that's not necessarily fear but rather a considered decision based on weighing up time versus income. Maybe I'm fearless!

IF YOU HAVE THE WORLD'S ATTENTION FOR 30 SECONDS, WHAT IS THAT YOU WOULD LIKE TO SAY?
Stop judging people!

arts *to* hearts
MAGAZINE

An Art publication with a mission to Discover, Connect, and Engage with Contemporary & Emerging Women Artists From around the world.

A Product of

ARTS TO HEARTS PROJECT

We are a global creative community uniting contemporary & emerging women Artists to build successful, fulfilling, and money-making careers via collaboration, learning, community, networking, and peer-to-peer learning.

SUBMIT YOUR WORK

We have several opportunities throughout the year for people interested in the global arts. From open calls to grants to exhibits, you can stay on top of all our upcoming and ongoing opportunities by subscribing to our newsletter on our website.

BACK COVER ART

Rithika Merchant | Solar Syncretism 2021 | 100 x 70 cms / 39.3 x 27.5 in | Gouache, watercolour and ink on paper

JOIN WOMEN ARTISTS WORLD WIDE BY ATH
www.facebook.com/groups/
womenartistsworldwideath/

VISIT OUR WEBSITE
www.artstoheartsproject.com

FOLLOW US ON INSTAGRAM
@artstoheartsproject

EMAIL
info@artstoheartsproject.com

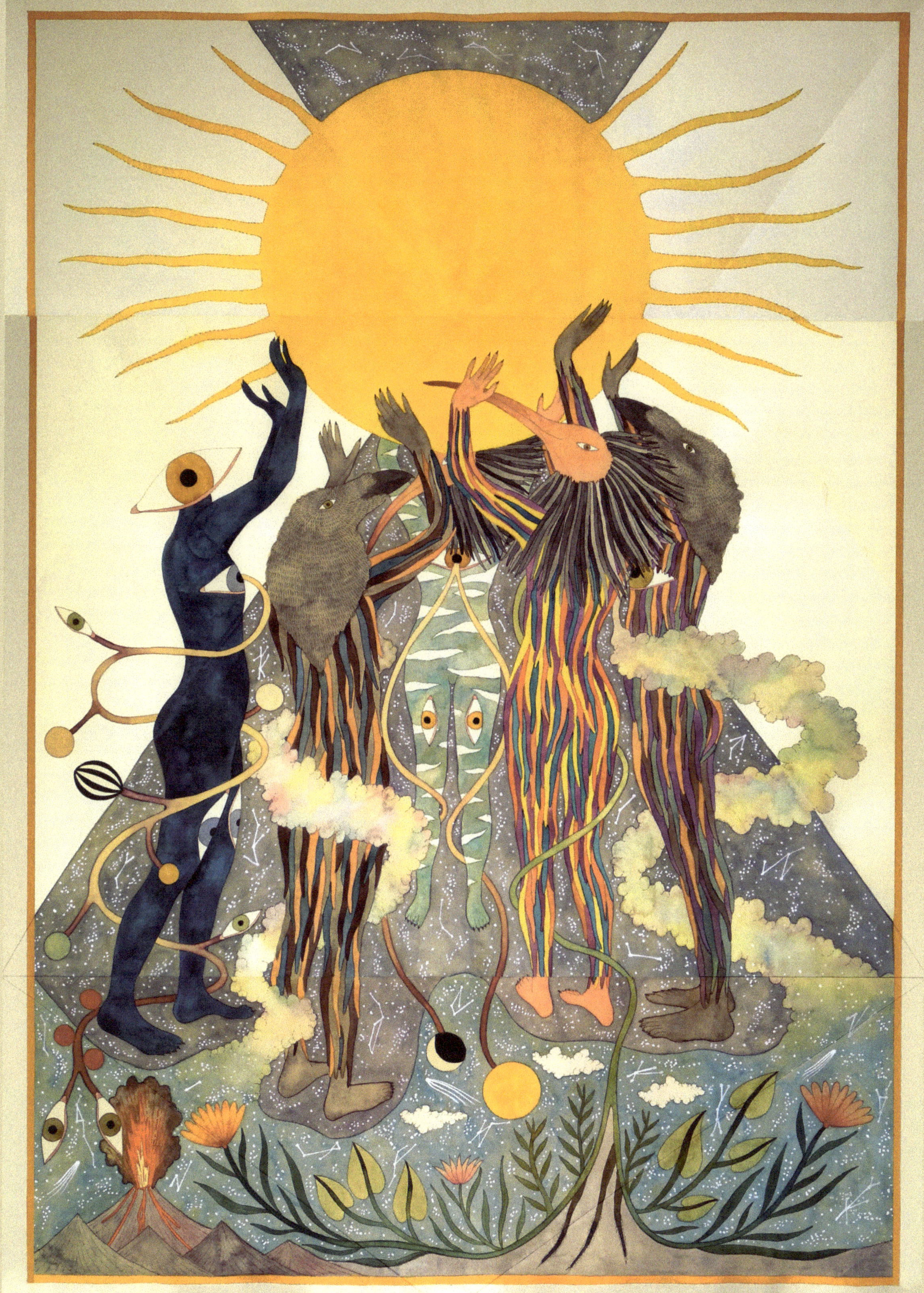